WAVES OF MAGIC

WAVES OF MAGIC

HOW TO TAP YOUR INNER RESOURCES TO ACHIEVE ANYTHING YOU WANT

PETER SASÍN

COPYRIGHT © 2018 PETER SASÍN
All rights reserved.

WAVES OF MAGIC
How to Tap Your Inner Resources to Achieve Anything You Want

ISBN 978-1-5445-1021-7 *Paperback*
       978-1-5445-1020-0 *Ebook*

Dedicated to you, the reader, for choosing to improve your life. By doing so, you make the world a better place. Thank you.

CONTENTS

ACKNOWLEDGMENTS 9

INTRODUCTION 11

1. CLARITY: HOW TO EXPRESS WHAT YOU WANT 31

2. M—MAGNETIZING PURPOSE AND PASSION: WHY DO YOU WANT WHAT YOU WANT? 53

3. A—ALL SENSES: YOUR TIME MACHINE 79

4. G—GPS: THE MAP TO THE LIFE YOU WANT........................97

5. I—INSPIRED ACTION: THE VEHICLE THAT TAKES YOU TO YOUR FUTURE LIFE 113

6. C—CREATE THE WAVES: CONSISTENT ACTION LEADS TO CONSTANT GROWTH...143

CONCLUSION 157

ABOUT THE AUTHOR 165

ACKNOWLEDGMENTS

I want to thank the following people:

Dr. Richard Bandler for your life's work and for providing me the most valuable lessons and skills in my life.

Kathleen and John LaValle for your passionate support and encouragement.

Marc A. Pletzer and Wiebke Lüth for your masterful way of bringing joy and competency into my work.

My Dream Team of Life Poets: You are amazing guys. You help me make my work easier and more meaningful.

A great Thank You to my love Ivetka for being my Soulmate and Lifesaving Angel. Without you, there is no me.

INTRODUCTION

WELCOME TO THE WAVE

COME ON IN; the water's fine. Most people show up believing that life isn't fair and they'll never reach their goals. If you have similar beliefs, I'm about to challenge them with magic—*waves and waves* of it.

Or maybe you already know that *life can be easy!*—but you think you don't know where to start. In that case, too, you happen to be in the *ideal* place. This book will show you that endless resources live inside of you; you need only to tap into them. It's actually easy to do.

"Yeah, sure," you may be thinking; you've heard that one before. So many people before me have promised you the moon. How is this book different? *It will teach you to use what you already possess.* When you do, you will be like the

Wright brothers, who combined widely available resources in a whole new way to build the machine that achieved the world's first piloted, sustained flight.[1]

The book adds the essential method and motivation. Even if you haven't experienced one of my seminars and you're skeptical, congratulations on opening the book. You're showing your understanding that it's not too late for your life to change—and you're right!

Let's start this adventure by exploring the metaphor of the Wave. It will help if you visualize yourself standing at the edge of the sea, so I'll set the stage: Hot sand covers your bare feet while waves roar in your ears and salt-misted air fills your lungs. As you're standing there, imagine you can see all the world in front of you in the form of a huge Wave. If you think big, you'll see all of humanity—billions of people—as part of the infinite energy of the Wave.

If you were to observe the inhabitants of this huge Wave, you would see that most people complicate their ride. Their hands and legs flail as they try to swim against the Wave. They inhale and gulp water, so they can't breathe as they crash into others in the same predicament. They try desperately to cling to these random meetings, while

---

[1] Smithsonian National Air and Space Museum, https://airandspace.si.edu/exhibitions/wright-brothers/online/

new screaming, fighting, kicking people constantly show up to bounce against them.

Some of those fighters, pushy as hell, manage to succeed—but not without injury, exhaustion, and climbs on the backs of their ever-changing neighbors. The others then worship them as heroes. These chosen ones spend the rest of their lives talking about their long, hard path to success.

This popular narrative only reinforces the myths of the Wave's unpredictability, unfairness, and difficulty. So we keep struggling while casting envious eyes on the conquerors.

Another group of inhabitants lets the Wave decide the course of their lives. Instead of fighting the Wave, they float passively and helplessly in it. Hoping to incur no injury, they only fail to make any progress.

Keep looking into the Wave, and amid all that chaos, you'll discover a third group—a different one. Like surfers, they joyfully ride the energy of the Wave. They set a flexible course and actively choose their companions—often fellow surfers. They're easy to spot in the crowd.

Study the surfers, and you'll also discover a principle that's foreign to the fighters and the floaters. It's the ability to use the power and the magic of the Wave.

Now tell me: Which type *are* you? Which type do you *want* to be?

I arrived at this understanding, appropriately enough, while I was standing on a literal beach. Watching wave after wave reach the shore, it suddenly struck me: Waves keep coming whether I or anyone else notices them or not.[2] Nothing about nature is random or chaotic. If we acknowledge her perfect rhythms, we can follow her lead. She is so precise, in fact, that you can set your watch by the sun and design a calendar based on the moon.

Living in chaos, on the other hand, works against nature. *Chaos* can be defined as the opposite of *cosmos*, which itself derives from a Greek word meaning both "universe" and a universe that's "orderly," "harmonious," and "systematic."[3]

Which will it be for you—cosmos or chaos? In this book, you'll learn how to understand and use nature's energy and the feedback that life sends you every day to create your most fulfilling life. It's a myth that a great opportunity comes along only once in your life. You don't have to spend energy regretting the one that got away. Don't

---

[2] As an example of things that we often disregard, did you notice that airplane windows each contain a tiny hole in the bottom? You didn't? Few people do because it's almost invisible. But it's doing a huge, maybe lifesaving job. They're there to balance inside and outside pressure and keep the window in place and intact.

[3] https://www.merriam-webster.com/dictionary/cosmos

wait any longer, though; take action *now*. Time is your most valuable resource.

OPEN UP TO MAGIC

Hold a space open for the possibility of good things so you can recognize them when they show up, unlike Wayne, a butcher featured in a United Kingdom video show about luck.[4] Wayne self-identified as unlucky and claimed that bad things always happened to him. In fact, bad things *had* happened to him, including getting shot in the nose when the car he was driving got in the way of a stray bullet.

Wayne so expected bad outcomes that when the luck researchers left a winning scratch-off lottery ticket at his door on purpose, he never knew he had won—he threw it away unscratched. When they deliberately put a fifty-pound bill in his path on the street, he didn't see it.

As I would have told Wayne, and as this book will show you, your thoughts create your reality. If a person believes he can't trust people, he'll see nothing but evidence to support that belief. A trusting person, on the other hand, sees the opposite. They're *both* right. Each is creating his own reality, individually interpreting the opportunities and lessons that arrive as regularly as the ocean's waves.

---

[4] "The Secret of Luck," 2011, an episode of *The Experiments*, a United Kingdom television series by mentalist Derren Brown, https://www.youtube.com/watch?v=O4mN33w5Ftw.

If you view yourself as unlucky, you probably find it hard to believe that opportunities keep coming. Luck has nothing to do with it, though. You make your so-called luck by being ready for the opportunities that continue to arrive. That person you meet on the train might be your next business or life partner. Whatever your age or your circumstances, you always have the chance to do or change something.

WAX YOUR SURFBOARD

If you can get beyond any limiting beliefs ("I'm too old," "I'm not good enough," "I'm too...[whatever]") and recognize the feedback you're receiving, you can always move forward. Take learning languages. Because my native language is Slovak, two years ago I couldn't imagine publishing even a single English sentence, let alone an entire book.

Even though I have no special linguistic ability, I now know I can master any language in the world. I credit the magic that's available to all of us, including you. By tapping into it, I learned English the easy and fun way—another lesson this book will teach you.

In this book, I'll also explain how to interpret the feedback life gives you. I'll show you how to multiply your energy by tapping into the power of the Wave. I'll also show you how—and how not—to talk with your subconscious. You'll learn that you don't have to struggle.

REALLY?

If that idea doesn't seem plausible, it's probably because you were conditioned to believe that life *is* a struggle and that only a life of struggle has value. When I asked you which Wave dweller you want to be, maybe your conscious mind answered "surfer" while you subconsciously might have chosen to struggle.

Maybe you're afraid *not* to struggle. If you dream of being rich, for example, part of you might actually fear it. Fairy tales and subsequent narratives taught you that the rich are evil and the poor are heroes. If you harbor a belief that wealth equals evil, your subconscious, part of whose job it is to protect you, will fight it relentlessly.

You'll need to update—reprogram—your beliefs because they enormously affect your life. Your reward for reprogramming them is also enormous: You can be a hero without suffering.

WHAT YOU'LL LEARN

I'll introduce you to a model I call the M.A.G.I.C. Reality Creator™. I developed it by observing life and the laws of nature. Understanding the model will show that the energy of the Wave is always available to you. If we use the energy to behave, believe, and even talk effectively, the outcome is guaranteed. The model will brighten your outlook, as I've demonstrated in work with my clients and myself. It will help you deepen your awareness and understand the feedback life hands you.

When we experience pain, a common type of feedback, it starts to feel expected and familiar; we quickly learn to tolerate it either by medicating or adapting. *Don't.* Instead, my model teaches you to see the pain as the tough-love messenger it is. It's telling you loud and clear to change something. As a simple example, if your head hurts because you're hitting it against the wall, don't take a painkiller. Stop hitting your head!

Feedback-driven change is up to you—not that wall, not the government, not your parents, not your boss. Assigning guilt can prevent you from taking full control of your life. Take responsibility for your feelings, your earnings, the quality of your relationships, and so on. Ask yourself, "What feedback do I want to feel instead?" Like many people, you may have trouble answering that question. The next chapter will help you.

SETTING YOUR FUTURE

You have probably experienced that setting goals is no guarantee of achieving results at all. If your goal is learning how to set goals, though, this book will support it.

What this book *won't* do is tell you to work harder or faster, like a hamster on a wheel. It also won't support any belief that you won't really live until you reach your goals. Does any variation of this statement feel familiar? "I can't be happy until I _____" (fill in the blank) buy this car, meet my life partner, live in that house, travel to Paris. In that way, goals can become excuses for deferring happiness.

I don't want you to repeat what hasn't worked a thousand times before. I won't ask you to follow the boring process that everyone else is teaching, such as making to-do lists. Why would I? You never wrote down some of the most important lessons you've ever learned—how to speak your native language, how to walk, and how to eat.

If you still want to set goals, though, I won't stop you. I'll ask only that you avoid deferring happiness and that you consider the goals as only a part of the future you'll envision for yourself. What we'll do in this book goes well beyond. Adapting a popular adage, I would suggest that where setting a goal is like *buying* a fish, mastering the M.A.G.I.C. Reality Creator™ is like *learning* to fish.

You'll also have to look elsewhere if you want a book on positive thinking. Often, when people follow such a practice, nothing changes. For example, consider someone who stays in a bad relationship by clinging to the small benefits. Instead, my model is grounded in honesty and clarity, which we'll explore in the next chapter.

To make needed changes, you need to see clearly what needs to change. Take in the feedback life hands you. If the Wave is hitting you hard in the face, pay attention. It's shouting at you to change, not to complain bitterly about life's brutality and not to accept it.

You can achieve all that transformation without suffering. In fact, you're likely to find yourself having fun. The lessons you'll learn in this book and the changes they'll provoke—if you're consistent about using them—are playful and easy. Yes, you heard it right. I know it's popular at the moment to say that no great achievement can come easily. I'll show in this book that ease is in fact the best course for your life and for this planet.

WHERE MY JOURNEY BEGAN

Although Waves are part of nature, finding and using them doesn't necessarily come naturally. In the same way, surfers at the beach must learn the basics: how to choose the right board, jump on, and ride the wave.

Riding the Wave certainly didn't come naturally to me. At one point in my life, I was doing menial jobs I didn't like, one after another. Working was about earning enough money to survive. After work, I would drink a few beers and watch some TV. My life was okay—no catastrophes to report—but I lived without purpose, structure, or service. I was wasting my energy and potential.

Then one day a friend asked me, "What would you do if you could? What would make you happy?" It was the first time anyone had asked me such questions, and for a moment, I had no answers. Then came a breakthrough: A thought bubbled up, and I said, "I want to play ice hockey." When my friend asked me how I would achieve that, he inspired me to research and act upon my dream.

I started to practice hockey, and my dream expanded: I wanted to play on the hockey team of the university where I was enrolled.[5] I was awful, but after two years of training, I not only earned a place on the team but also soon became a hockey coach on the team. At thirty years old, I had fulfilled a dream for the first time in my life. Although I didn't know it, I had found magic.

After I realized how easy it was to succeed, for the first time *I* started asking myself the big questions: "What do you want from the future? What do you want from your *life*?"

---

5   Ludwig-Maximilians-Universität München (LMU)

Those questions then stopped me in my tracks. I had been a master at escaping from future-setting chats. This time, though, my mind couldn't let go of the questions. I began searching for answers in personal-development books.

Each book made me hungry for more knowledge. When a few books mentioned neuro-linguistic programming (NLP), I became curious: "What is this NLP stuff?" I started reading every book I could find on NLP communication—including spoken, thought, and body language—which hugely influenced my life.

I also started dreaming about the future. I experienced my first result when I dreamed of working for a specific company a few months before I actually landed the job.

After immersing myself in books and seminars about NLP and other teachings, I eventually transformed from a guy who feared the future to one who trains others to create their best future. In 2012, I formed a company to help others take control of their lives.

FINDING MAGIC

I couldn't stop thinking about why so many adults believe that life must be a struggle. Young children know better. Watch them learn to walk: They fall, they laugh, and they get up again. The process isn't painful because they observe the outcome by watching other people walk. How great it would be, I reasoned, if adults could adopt the strategy we once knew.

As it turns out, we can adopt that strategy. I tested the model on myself, and I shared it with my clients and seminar attendees; we all experienced its magic.

In this book, you'll learn that my M.A.G.I.C. Reality Creator™ is about fulfilling your purpose. I developed the model from my desire to replace pain with joy and ease in the process of transformation. It doesn't have to be hard.

The model contains five parts, each represented in the acronym and in a chapter of its own:

Chapter One: Clarity Leads to **M.A.G.I.C.**
Chapter Two: **M**agnetizing Purpose and Passion
Chapter Three: **A**ll Senses
Chapter Four: **G**PS
Chapter Five: **I**nspired Action
Chapter Six: **C**reate the Waves

The model has the potential to help you dramatically change your life—for the better. Its parts will show you how to talk about and clearly visualize your desired outcomes.[6] Bringing clarity to your dreams helps your subconscious navigate to your passion and purpose.

---

6 You probably already use visualization. However, this book will show you how to visualize four times more powerfully.

The same way that creating one's future differs from setting goals, the M.A.G.I.C. Reality Creator™ differs from the S.M.A.R.T. model you may be familiar with. S.M.A.R.T.—which stands for goals that are Specific, Measurable, Achievable, Realistic, and Timely—is a model for improving performance, often in work teams. Although M.A.G.I.C. also works for teams, I designed it to help individuals achieve a better future. It opens doors to a higher level of life.

What the S.M.A.R.T. model doesn't do is determine that people are doing what they love. Consider the three main differences between the models:

1. M.A.G.I.C. respects your energy, values, and purpose. (Remember that hamster wheel I mentioned earlier? M.A.G.I.C. helps you surf the Waves, not trap you on a wheel or a treadmill.)
2. M.A.G.I.C. supports your vision and dreams. When Richard Branson[7] creates his vision for the future, he exemplifies M.A.G.I.C., even if he isn't yet familiar with the term. He not only innovates, but he also clearly enjoys what he's doing, and he values his staff and his audiences. S.M.A.R.T., on the other hand,

---

[7] I refer to Richard Branson here instead of Steve Jobs, who is often mentioned as a paragon of vision. It's true that Jobs achieved a brilliant vision for the future of technology, and I enjoy owning Apple products. Because of how he treated the people around him, though, I wouldn't call him a practitioner of M.A.G.I.C. When people lead by terror instead of love, they exact a high energetic cost. Jobs didn't seem to know that people are always more important than products.

helps with achieving other people's dreams. The work of Branson's *staff* toward his vision might be more in that category.

3. M.A.G.I.C. has no parallel to the "T" in the S.M.A.R.T. model. The problem with using time is that it motivates externally, often arbitrarily and ineffectually. For example, if you were to set a timeline to become a millionaire in five years, how would you know you could not achieve it in two? Or if you think you might be able to achieve the same goal in seven years, you might stall for two years, thinking, "Oh, I have plenty of time left!"

There's another problem with time as a motivator of your future life, as opposed to the completion of a team project. People often use a deadline—and notice the first part of that word—as an excuse not to take action right away. M.A.G.I.C., on the other hand, employs more powerful *internal* motivators.

NO DREAM TOO BIG

Anyone and any dream can benefit from M.A.G.I.C. Consider Rado, a client who uses a wheelchair because he broke his neck and was paralyzed in an accident so traumatic he can't recall it. He remembers only hearing the doctor say he'll never again be able to move any part of his body below his neck. Rado refused to accept that life sentence. When he and his aide listened to my podcast and attended my seminars, he began to transform from the inside out, using his inner resources.

Despite the doctor's prognosis, Rado can now move his hands and arms, and he can drive a car. As I write this, he can't yet walk—another of his dreams—but I'm absolutely certain he will.

How did Rado transform? He allowed me to expose him to M.A.G.I.C. That doesn't mean I stood over him, uttering voodoo incantations while circling my hands around. I merely showed him how to process his thoughts and take appropriate actions. He did the work, and he did it easily.

M.A.G.I.C. can help you whatever your goals, which are possibly different from Rado's. Maybe you want great relationships. Maybe you crave more professional success or a job you love. Maybe you want glowing health. Maybe you want to (drumroll) find and fulfill your purpose in life. Or maybe you don't know what you want, except that it's not what you have now.

Whatever it is that you dream of, you probably also want to stop struggling, a worthy goal in itself, because struggling consumes enormous amounts of energy.

YOU CAN CHANGE YOUR LIFE

I don't promise that reading this book or even attending my seminars will change your life. Reading and attending aren't enough. They weren't enough to cause Rado's transformation. As he did, you must *use* what you learn, because change is up to you.

You don't even have to agree with me about everything. I'm asking you only to bring curiosity and an open mind to experiment with new ideas, including the ones in this book. Words have power to affect our actions, so I use the verbs *experiment*, *do*, and *test* rather than *try* because they imply action and completion. By contrast, if you say, "I tried to open the door," it sounds as though you didn't succeed.

Test the problem with the verb *try* for yourself with this exercise:

1. Close your eyes and imagine a heavy metal sphere in front of you, and *try* to lift it.
2. Let's start again. Close your eyes and imagine the same heavy metal sphere in front of you. Now lift it!

Could you lift the sphere at least once? If so, which time? Most people who do the exercise find it easy to lift only the second time. In fact, half of them can't even budge it. That tiny word *try* can make us weak! That's why I use it carefully or not at all.

CONTINUE TO EXPERIMENT ON YOURSELF

Like words, thoughts hold enormous power. They not only influence actions, but they also change our DNA. Knowing that fact might interest you and satisfy the logic side of your brain. Like other science-based facts, though, it won't necessarily help you change your thoughts and your life. That's why I haven't packed the book with scientific data, which is based only on other people's experiences.

Let me clarify. You'll continue to find examples of my and other people's individual experiences in the book as sources of inspiration. What you won't find, though, are quantitative results, such as "Seventy-five percent of participants showed this reaction to that stimulus." Instead, you'll change your life by having, interpreting, and using your own experiences. This book's many exercises will turn *you* into the scientist conducting experiments on *yourself*.

YOUR JOURNEY STARTS NOW

Whether or not you're aware of it, you're already in the Wave. If you're comfortable with suffering or drifting in it, this book is not for you. But if you want to learn how to be successful and master your life with ease, stay with me. You don't have to struggle or drift; it's easier and far more satisfying to ride the Wave. Change is possible, no matter how desperate life may feel right now. As a human being, you're designed to thrive. If you believe in magic and you're ready to change, you're exactly where you need to be.

Are you ready?

CHAPTER 1

CLARITY: HOW TO EXPRESS WHAT YOU WANT

"BE CLEAR ABOUT what you want."

I know, I know—you've heard it about a thousand times before, in every book and seminar. The problem is that you can't be clear about what you want until you understand what clarity really is. So many misconceptions exist. Ironically, clarity hasn't been made *clear*.

There's another obstacle people often face when they even think about being clear about desires. Not everybody is ready to believe that life can be easy. For many people, it's a new, strange idea, and we can leave it aside for the moment. Before you dive into what M.A.G.I.C. can do for you, you must decide what you *want* it to do for you. For example, where do you want to be in five years? What do you want? What would make you happy?

Boom! Maybe even answering those questions seems as impossible as believing in an easy life. You'll find clarity in this chapter, including suggestions that will probably surprise you. For one thing, you won't need to take notes or make lists.

DON'T MESS WITH "DON'T"

Let's start by brushing away a common misunderstanding. If you ask people what they want, many often tell you what they *don't* want: "I don't want to be poor." "I don't want to be ill." "I don't want to work for that person anymore."

Those people *think* they've effectively expressed their desire. To the *conscious* mind, "I don't want to be poor" and "I want to be rich" are the same. To the *subconscious* mind, though, the statements are *not* the same. When people express their desires using negative terms like *not*, *no*, or *nothing*, the speakers' inner resources can't help.

It's as if you go into a restaurant, and when the server asks you what you want for lunch, you say, "I don't want a burger, I don't want pasta, and I don't want a salad." When he replies, "That narrows it down a bit, but what

BE CLEAR ABOUT WHAT YOU WANT.

is it you want?" you insist you've already told him. The customer is always right, so he returns from the kitchen with calf's liver. If his selection does not please you, would you complain that you didn't get what you wanted?

Most people know not to behave that way in a restaurant, but they do when they're "ordering" aspects of their lives. They sort of play Russian roulette, but worse (well, except for the possibility of getting killed). The outcome is often exactly what they said they didn't want. For example, my friend from college dreamed of a future husband who was not short, blond, or a soldier. Today she is married to a short, blond cop. (YES! He's not a soldier! Close enough, though—*damn*.)

If we consider the nature of our subconscious minds, my friend's outcome should have been obvious. We so often get what we expressly don't want because the subconscious skips the negative words, such as *not*. The mind knows only how to add things, not to remove them. For example, if I ask you *not* to imagine an alarm clock in a refrigerator, it's likely that you instantly call up a vivid image.

When I pose that question in seminars, attendees of all ages usually describe an old-fashioned clock with two bells on top in an empty refrigerator. People tend to add similar details to their "forbidden" images.[1] We are capable of "seeing" something, like an alarm clock in a fridge, that we've never actually seen.[2] We can imagine, say, being happy or being rich even if we've never been happy or rich before. Our minds are remarkable.

Our minds imagine so they can process information. You might have experienced telling a child not to do something—such as "Don't climb that tree because you'll fall"—only to watch her disobey. The child was likely to do so for a reason that's all in her mind. You planted an idea she could understand only by imagining climbing the tree and falling. Whether or not she fell, or even actually climbed, the movie you programmed in her head will replay whenever it fits.

To send the right message to our subconscious, we need to clarify our dreams and how we express them.[3]

BE SPECIFIC

Along with being positive, the information that we send

---

[1] Just between us, is there a chance you added similar details to your "forbidden" image?

[2] Well, a reader of my article in a business magazine reported seeing an *actual* alarm clock in her refrigerator. She had literally put it there to stop its loud ticking from disturbing her sleep.

[3] If you've reached this point in the chapter without being able to identify your deepest desires, you might first need to persuade yourself that you're entitled to them. Of course, you are, but your background might have taught you otherwise. Your first M.A.G.I.C. act might be to visualize yourself as someone who believes you deserve your dreams. It will also help to practice suspending disbelief.

to our subconscious also must be specific. For example, if you tell your mind that you want more money—a popular wish—you need to illustrate exactly what that means. Otherwise, find a penny on the street, and your subconscious reacts, "Mission accomplished!" You might have gained only a penny, but it's still *more money* than you had before. The subconscious mind tends to be that literal. That's the way it fulfills the wishes in all areas of your life.

Instead, paint the picture of what the experience of having enough money would be like. Imagine where you would live, what you would drive, what you would wear, and where you would travel. Imagine how your life would look if you had all the money you want today.

PLAN YOUR OUTCOME, NOT THE PROCESS

Although many people begin a life change by planning a series of steps, the process is not the right place to start. Considering process *is* important, although defining your desired outcome—or goal—must come first. (Later in the book, we'll look at the process stage but in a different way than you might expect. You won't find any requirement to make lists in the process I recommend.)

The problem with a step-by-step process is that it can hinder flexibility. In fact, starting with the process rather than the outcome is one of the most common causes of failure. For example, if your desired outcome is to win a contract with a certain company, the first step of a process might be to call the CEO's assistant. If he doesn't give out the number or the CEO doesn't want to meet, though, you're stuck at step one. Focus on the outcome instead, and you're far more apt to beat any obstacle to getting there.

Along with focusing on the outcome, you'll strengthen your visualization if you add the "scenario" dimension. Where an outcome might be buying your dream house, the scenario is imagining a future in that house. You might picture your family happily living there, maybe celebrating a birthday or hosting a holiday feast.

To further explain the difference between the goal or outcome and the scenario, let's say you're facing a meeting with potential clients. You focus on the outcome if you expect to have a good meeting. You visualize the scenario if you imagine yourself shaking hands, brilliantly answering clients' questions, and hearing them offer you their business.

When I prepare for a speech before a large audience, my *goal* is to give a great speech. To support that goal, I imagine the *scenario* of a standing ovation, followed by audience members approaching me to sign their copy of my book. Reality often reflects my visualizations, so

I credit them with at least part of the reason for that happy ending.

MORE EXAMPLES OF CLARITY IN ACTION

The M.A.G.I.C. Reality Creator™ has endless applications. In this section, we'll explore some typical situations, including those shared by my seminar attendees.

TRANSFORMING IN-LAW VISITS

Maybe you're concerned about an upcoming visit from your in-laws (if you adore yours or if you don't have any, just play along). Based on previous visits, you might start thinking, "Man, this visit will be a *disaster!*" That expectation, especially as expressed, is likely to be a self-fulfilling prophecy.

Setting a more positive goal—let's say, a good relationship with your in-laws—will work better, but even that doesn't go far enough. You should also imagine what that future relationship would look and feel like (and any other appropriate senses, all of which we'll explore in Chapter Three).

At this point, you might be thinking, "What's he talking about? It's impossible to imagine a good relationship with my in-laws!" I'll ask you to suspend disbelief, as if you're making a fictional movie. Maybe you imagine a scene in which you greet them with warm hugs and praise; maybe you see yourselves enjoying preparing meals together and, after they return home, calling each other just to chat. These thoughts will change your state of mind and possibly your in-laws'. The change will help you actually look forward to their next visit.

TRANSFORMING DINNER WITH THE KIDS

Another typical family situation that can need improvement is daily dinner with one's children. You, like many parents I hear from, might dream of children who, instead of fighting, sit quietly and eat or who answer your many questions about their day. The first dream would probably bore the children, though, and the second is likely to strike them as gestapo-like.

In that case, I would advise you to redesign your scenario to make everyone happy. For example, you might imagine everyone having a good conversation. Picture the light in your children's faces as they have fun sharing their secrets. Hear everyone's laughter, and feel the warmth and the joy.

TRANSFORMING "SO SAD!"

When a seminar attendee and his wife walked in the neighborhood, he said people often stopped to admire their one-year-old son. If the boy was not smiling when they peered into the stroller, they would say something like, "Is he sad?" After the first time, the experience repeated itself, and the father asked me what to say to make the onlookers stop making such comments.

I counseled him, "Go back a step. By the time the onlookers react, it's too late to change the scenario." Their feedback was influencing the parents' behavior toward the child; the parents started to approach him as a sad child. That approach, in turn, influenced the child's behavior.

I advised him instead to prepare *before* the walk for a different outcome. If he and his wife could imagine a favorable scenario, one in which passersby praise the child for beautifully smiling, they could replace the negative image. The parents would react to their son as though he were a happy child. That alone, I said, would manifest smiles all around.

The man and his wife, although skeptical, went to work on this simple idea. First, they needed to become aware of the times they thought of their son as frowning. Then they substituted smiling images. As I had counseled, they employed various senses to add details to the mental picture. For example, they imagined the weather, feeling the sun on their skin, and the sounds in the neighborhood.

When I met the man a few months later, he said the situation had dramatically changed almost immediately. When *they*, the boy's parents, stopped letting themselves be influenced by other people's reactions to the child's sad face, their new perspective triggered a new reality. The way they approached the child now resulted in a happy expression, and spectators' comments reflected it. The parents had planned and created this exact outcome.

TRANSFORMING PHOBIAS

Future-scenario images can also sometimes help combat phobias. For example, another client asked how to cure her daughter's fear of the subway. I advised the client to imagine her child laughing in the subway car. When the mother projected that image onto the child in the form of new behavior, she stopped expecting a terrible subway experience and allowed the child to release her fear.

TRANSFORMING ATHLETIC PERFORMANCE

Let's also take the example of athletes. When I ask them what they want, most athletes say only that they don't want to lose. So after turning that around—to "I want to win"—they can build future scenarios, as successful athletes do. Runners might see themselves dashing first through the finish line or wearing a gold medal; hockey players might see themselves scoring the winning goal. Of course, that doesn't mean they always win, because other factors weigh in, but they've done the essential subconscious work to set themselves to win.

Like the frowning baby's mother, you may be skeptical. Sometimes, seeing is believing. I again urge you to suspend disbelief long enough to put your heart into an experiment about something you want to change.[4]

PROVE IT YOURSELF

As you've already seen in this chapter, your subconscious mind can change your reality. It can change your reality *the way you want* if you speak clearly to it in a language it can understand. Now you might be ready for some proof beyond the examples I've already given you. I invite you to test the M.A.G.I.C. model; this book contains many experiments, and you can find more in my other book, *Triumph: Your New Life Story*,[5] and on www.wavesofmagic.com.

I test the model every day, both with my clients and by myself, in both small and big ways. For example, I had read about an experiment in Washington, DC, that illus-

---

[4] I'm not saying that clarity is the fix for everything. However, it *can* bring spectacular and rapid results. Whenever you're not happy with the feedback you get from life, start by asking, "What do I want instead?" and be damn specific.

[5] To find out when *Triumph: Your New Life Story* will be released in the United States, sign up for my newsletter at www.wavesofmagic.com. The book is the translation of my *TRIUMF: Váš nový životný príbeh* (published in Slovakia in 2014).

trates the power of M.A.G.I.C. During the two months that hundreds of people meditated on inner images of peace, the crime rate in that city dropped by 23.3 percent.[6] I repeated the experiment in Bratislava with the 250 people in my seminar.

When we looked at the official crime statistics for that Saturday, we compared them to the stats of the same day on many other weeks. The daily minimum was typical: nine crimes. On our meditative Saturday, though, the number fell, not to zero, but to three crimes, a 66 percent reduction. The result shows one of two things. Either it works to use thoughts to influence reality, or most of the criminals were in my seminar instead of committing crimes!

Although we can measure the crime rate, we can't count how many good things happened on meditation day—how many people felt inspired to help someone. Wouldn't it be wonderful if cities collected that type of data?

You don't have to change your city's crime rate to demonstrate the value of M.A.G.I.C., though, and you don't have to move the planets. You can start with something personal. For example, you could experiment on your next meeting with a potential client. Visualize how you want to feel during and after that meeting.

---

6   http://www.worldpeacegroup.org/washington_crime_study.html.

LISTENING TO ECHOES

If you're familiar with *The Secret* book or movie and its explanation of the Law of Attraction, you also might be wondering whether and how M.A.G.I.C. compares. I credit *The Secret* for preaching the power of the conscious mind and for inspiring people to think positively. It contends that what you think is what you experience.

On the other hand, the book and film seem to suggest that a wish alone is enough to change one's future. But wishing, which engages only the conscious mind, is only a micro step. It leaves out the subconscious mind, so it lacks inspired action on the part of the wisher.

Like *The Secret*, the M.A.G.I.C. model encourages you to view the Universe—and your life—as the great echo machine that it is. In both models, the Universe delivers feedback based on what your subconscious calls in. M.A.G.I.C., though, gives you more tools to understand that feedback and react appropriately to it.

The question is this: Do you love the feedback you're getting? If you don't, it's futile to complain about the feedback. It's even more futile to ignore the feedback and repeat the failure. That repetition might even be *insane*, according to one definition.[7]

---

[7] "Insanity: doing the same thing over and over again and expecting different results." By Unknown: brainyquotes.com.

Instead, use the feedback, and if you don't like it, consider what you can change. For example, illness is often nothing more than feedback. You probably have family members, friends, or acquaintances who recovered after responding to the feedback by changing something, whether behavior, environment, or beliefs.

PICTURING YOUR FUTURE

When you think about your future, *how* do you see it? Many people find it surprising that their minds often use pictures to process their thoughts. What's more, image-based thoughts aren't limited to sighted people. Even people who have been blind since birth use a type of visual interpretation to process thoughts. In their case in particular, hearing and touch tend to inform their images.

The power of visualization suggests why you *read about* visualization in so many goal-oriented books. *How* you visualize makes all the difference to the quality of the outcome. Returning to the money goal, someone who always thinks about not wanting to be poor shouldn't expect the mind to be able to call up pictures of wealth. The mind can't turn "not poor" into "wealthy" images. Our minds and our lives can go only in the direction determined by the pictures we feed them. The M.A.G.I.C. model adds precision to the mental images.

Because it speaks so clearly to the subconscious, M.A.G.I.C. also helps you *apply* its lessons on a subconscious level. This model, unlike those that address only your conscious mind, is unlikely to fade with time. Like a baby who, having learned to walk, doesn't return to crawling, you'll continue to practice these subconscious communication skills. It's as if you're rewired.

The story of a client further illustrates the rarity of a relapse after using the M.A.G.I.C. model. This man was agoraphobic[8] until he learned how to speak to his subconscious mind, which didn't only improve his symptoms—it permanently cured him.

You've probably heard the expression, "Be careful what you wish for; you just might get it." M.A.G.I.C.'s version is "Be careful what you show and tell your subconscious because you *will* get it."

NOT FOR EVERYONE? NONSENSE!

The M.A.G.I.C. Reality Creator™ is easy and radically effective, so why doesn't everyone use it? First, everyone doesn't know about it yet. Second, some people who *do* know about it don't trust what they haven't experienced. To other people, it sounds like voodoo. To the second and

---

8   Agoraphobia is an anxiety disorder. My client feared leaving his home.

BE CAREFUL WHAT YOU SHOW AND TELL YOUR SUBCONSCIOUS BECAUSE YOU *WILL* GET IT.

third groups, I say, "Skip the excuses! Test the model! You have nothing to lose and everything to gain!"

Related to the second group are the people who insist, "How can I imagine being a millionaire? I can't picture what I haven't seen!" The alarm-clock-in-the-fridge example demonstrates you can. In your mind at this moment are the images of a version of yourself who is more successful, more beloved, happier, and richer than you are now. Let's pull them out of you. If you still feel an absence of images, though, just pretend how it would feel if you *could* imagine. What would you observe?

A final group tested the model without seeing desired results. That happened for one or more of three reasons: Their images weren't clear enough, they didn't pay close enough attention to the feedback they were receiving, or they *tried* instead of testing.

RECAPPING CLARITY

To get ready to meet the M.A.G.I.C. Reality Creator™ in detail, let's go over the steps to achieving clarity:

1. Focus on the outcome, not the process.
2. Ask yourself, "What outcome do I want instead of

what I have now?" If you don't know the answer, keep asking until you get it.[9]

3. Next, tackle "How will I know when I get it?" That question should trigger another series of questions related to scenarios. For example, how would you know that your sales prospect is happy? How would she look and what would she say if she wants to meet again?

4. Working backward from the happy end state, create images that illustrate it. An example is the athlete who starts with wearing a gold medal after crossing the finish line. Because trainers and authors often ask you to focus on the process, this step may seem counterintuitive to you. It isn't to your subconscious, though.

For example, if you're looking for the love of your life, picture a perfect future for you and him or her before imagining the path you might take to get to that point. How will you recognize it as a perfect future? You might say that you see the two of you relaxing, traveling, cooking, and attending events together. You might've gone on a lot of dates and signed up for every dating website, but if you haven't engaged your subconscious, you haven't done everything you can.

---

[9] Yes, it's really that simple! Just keep asking for as long as it takes. You may get your answer faster than you expect.

The saying "Fake it until you make it" applies here. I recommend that you further help your subconscious by making room in your life—your home—for someone else. That doesn't mean you need a big apartment, only that you clear some space in your closet and in the bathroom. Get rid of some things if you need to. If your soul mate appeared on your doorstep today, would you have room for that person?

One client had trouble finding a partner. When she mentioned that she loves going to the movies, I suggested that she buy a second ticket to tell her subconscious mind that she's not going alone. The client started to overthink: "Do I call a friend to use the ticket?" No, I said, just keep buying the extra ticket. One day, I added, her subconscious mind will see that she uses the spare.

The woman might have taken my advice; when I later ran into her at the gas station, she was with a man. I didn't ask, but he certainly appeared to be her significant other.

Just yesterday, a former seminar attendee told me he credits an extra toothbrush and cleared space in the closet with meeting the woman who became his wife.

Engaging the subconscious is not only easy, but it can also be a game. Trying too hard, on the other hand, can work against a quest for love, prospects, anything.

READY, SET, APPLY

In this chapter about clarity, you've learned how to clear the way to magic through the M.A.G.I.C. Reality Creator™. You've learned the need to express your desires in positive terms and as detailed scenarios visualized in your mind. In each of the next chapters, you'll learn the five magical steps to riding the Wave and bringing magic into your life.

CHAPTER 2

M–MAGNETIZING PURPOSE AND PASSION: WHY DO YOU WANT WHAT YOU WANT?

PERHAPS YOU KNOW PEOPLE who seem burned out by what they're doing. I think they're actually *bored* out. They're not following the advice of Warren Buffett, CEO of Berkshire Hathaway and perhaps the most successful investor of all time. Asked in an interview for his recipe for a joyful career, he responded, simply and without missing a beat, "Find your passion."[1]

---

[1] CNN Money interview, November 16, 2012, by Andrew Serwer when he was managing editor of *Fortune* magazine and Carol Loomis when she was senior editor-at-large at *Fortune*: http://money.cnn.com/video/magazines/fortune/2012/11/16/f-buffett-career-advice.fortune.

Of course, he's right, unlike people who think passion should take a back seat to facts and figures. I once heard that many bankers won't approve loans for passionate people, on the theory that those would-be borrowers might ignore business details. That idea sets up the misconception that you can have either passion or an eye on the bottom line, but not both. Passion isn't the problem in those cases, though—it's in the manner of communication. Have passion *and* be able to talk numbers with bankers.

As you learned in Chapter One, there's no substitute for being clear on your dream (and positive in how you think about it). Now that you understand the true meaning of clarity, you're ready to learn the model. It's time to look at the first step—the *M*—in the M.A.G.I.C. Reality Creator™. Magnetizing your purpose and passion is the message and the job of this chapter. Discover what magnetizes you.

Why have you chosen your dream? Examine the motivation behind it. If it begins with passion—if your dream is really what you want for yourself—you're on the right track. Conversely, if your dream lacks passion at its core, you're more likely to fail. Common misguided motivations include fame, admiration, praise, or glory.

I'm asking you to start by shining a light on what you love. Choose your dream *because* you love it, *not* because you expect people to love you for it.

CHOOSE YOUR DREAM BECAUSE YOU LOVE IT, NOT BECAUSE YOU EXPECT PEOPLE TO LOVE YOU FOR IT.

FOLLOW YOUR PASSION TO YOUR PURPOSE

I believe we each come into this world with a purpose, your higher mission—it's why you're on this planet and how you make the world a better place. We can discover and ultimately fulfill that purpose only through discovering our passion. Some people discover their passion as early as childhood. I once learned about a five-year-old sculptor whose mother said the sculptor had known what she wanted to do with her life since she was two years old.

Only a few people achieve this level of clarity so early in life, though. What's more, many of those who do find their passion don't practice it because some authority figure persuasively discourages them. "You can't make a living, raise a family, or pay off your loans doing that!" Does that sound familiar? It certainly does to me. Discouraged people often turn their backs on their passion and purpose in favor of a more "sensible" way of living.

Don't let it happen to you. *Claim* your birthright. If it already *has* happened to you, *re*claim it. It's no less than your *duty* to find your passion.

Consider it also your duty to use that passion to fulfill your purpose in life. You should know that not doing so is actually *selfish*. That's right. It's selfish because making excuses to avoid living your passion keeps you from sharing your true gifts with the world.

That idea will sound strange if you, like so many others, instead equate having big dreams—or even achieving happiness—with selfishness. One of my clients told me, "If I were happy, it would be unfair to unhappy people." That belief had held her back all her life. I asked her, "Is it unfair to you if someone else is happy?" She was quick to respond, "No! Of course not!" Only then did she understand that if she became happy, it would not harm anyone.

Maybe, like my client, you feel "okay" with your life because you think it would be selfish to aspire to more. But thinking *small* is what's selfish; small thinkers don't reach their full potential, which also means they can't serve as effective role models to people who have not reached theirs. Those are the actual goals of thinking big, rather than needing to build a fortune or an empire.

So, as I often say in my seminars, "If you want to make the world a better place, you had better know your gifts and share them." Showing people how to identify and share their gifts is my life's work.

MAGNETS HAVE TWO POLES

If you have any trouble recognizing what you're passionate about, identify your motivations. They come in two basic types, which are like magnetic poles. You can look at what pulls you toward what you want. Or you can focus

IF YOU WANT TO MAKE THE WORLD A BETTER PLACE, YOU HAD BETTER KNOW YOUR GIFTS AND SHARE THEM.

on the opposite type, which pushes you *away* from what you *don't* want. In fact, both types motivate you toward your passion, but in opposite ways.

To determine which type will work better for you, ask yourself, "What are the consequences of *not* following my passion?" If the answer resonates with you more than considering the outcome of following it, you've probably found your type.

In my case, I was motivated—*pulled*—toward writing this book by maintaining a positive mental image of how beautiful it would be. I visualized you holding the book and how it would change your life.

As an alternative, I might have found it helpful (but less fun) to imagine how bad it would be if I didn't write this book. I could have told myself something like, "Everybody except me is writing one" or "I'll never have the opportunity to help people throughout the world if I don't write one."

Many successful people combine these strategies at the same time, imagining the beauty of reaching their goals along with the pain of not doing so.

IDENTIFYING YOUR PURPOSE CAN TAKE TIME—AND TREATS

What does finding and living with passion and purpose look like? It's not always love at first sight. Consider Lilly, my beautiful Parson Russell Terrier. When she was a puppy, I took her to agility training, a timed obstacle-course sport for people and their dogs. On the first day, the trainer pointed out where we would start—if Lilly had not disappeared. Agility training didn't interest her at all; sniffing the yard was far more attractive to her.

Lilly's rude commentary on the sport discouraged me but not the trainer, who began to offer a reward, such as a bit of ham, for each leaped hurdle. It took several visits for Lilly to discover her passion for agility training. After that, she couldn't wait to start; she needed no prompting to run the obstacles by herself.

At the same time, Lilly inspired this lesson for you. Instead of doing something only once or twice, invest the time and energy to find and patiently nurture the seed of passion that *is* inside you. This seed doesn't live only in some favored few people. Because you're human, you possess it!

NURTURING THE SEED

For more proof that the seed can take time to grow, let's look at students of any musical instrument. At first, everything feels difficult. Then when they achieve some success, they can find themselves getting bored and ready to quit. Perseverance from that point on is likely to reveal either passion for the instrument or certainty of none.

New joggers experience a similar process. Most of them have sore muscles to show for their first workout. After jogging becomes a passion, though, it becomes more painful for them to imagine *not* jogging.

How long might it take to discover a new passion or habit? Theories range from twenty-one to sixty days, but my knowledge of psychology suggests it can happen in as little as a day or less. My seminar participants have been known to experience lasting change in mere *minutes*.

For example, during one of my recent weekend trainings, one woman thanked me for having taught her, three months earlier, a quick brain-reprogramming technique she used to control her eating habits. Not only had she lost more than sixty-five pounds, but she had also done it easily and sustainably. What's more, the pride in her eyes as she reported her achievement demonstrated her passion for her new lifestyle.

Success depends on the commitment of the individual, so of course I can't promise that everyone will achieve such dramatic results. The point, though, is how quickly she achieved them. The technique, based on our brain's abilities to quickly recognize and adapt patterns, takes less than twenty minutes to learn.

THE OPPOSITE OF LIVING WITH PASSION

Time works *against* a type of people I call "weekend zombies," who really live only two days each week. Monday is the most dreaded, depressing day of their week, which improves with each day. By Friday, these zombies feel like shouting "Yes!" because for most of the weekend, they know they can do what they want, which is often only eating and sleeping.

Weekend zombies live and work without passion and only for the money. They're one of those selfish groups I talked about earlier because if they inspire anyone for anything, it's only to avoid being a zombie! Seeing weekend zombies' unhappiness can show everyone else how not to live, so maybe *that's* zombies' purpose!

If you're a weekend zombie, planning for a happy life only when you retire, listen to this: your plans are bullshit. There is no happy end to an unhappy journey. To live the life of your dreams, change your life *now, wherever you are in it*. Even if you've already retired, it's not too late to find your passion. After retirement in her mid-sixties, one client found her passion of making beautiful scrapbooks and teaching the craft. She loves every day of her life. With her passion and gifts, she inspires people of all ages, acting as a role model for people who think they're too old to do anything. It's beautiful to watch her thrive.

WHAT IF EVERYONE DID WHAT THEY LOVE?

People often tell me, "Not everyone can be happy." My response is always, "How's that?" If everyone did what they love, the world would certainly be a happier place. Anyway, why should you concern yourself with "everyone?" People tend to worry too much about "What if everybody...?" questions instead of taking responsibility for their own lives. That's why I recommend that you start with yourself.

You also might wonder about jobs that don't necessarily inspire passion. What about them? Again, fake it until you make it; find some passion for the job. For example, I once worked as a dishwasher. The job wasn't my passion, but I did it with a *kind* of passion because I always worked at improving. For example, I challenged and taught myself to pull five dishes from the rack at once. None of my colleagues could do that.

More important than the jobs we do is how we think about—reframe—those jobs. Trash collection? Some trash collectors may think just that they have a stinky job while others may find passion in helping to keep the planet clean.

When I was little, my friends and I dreamed about driving a garbage truck or hanging from its rear handles. We thought the job was cool, so we would have been inspired trash collectors. We wouldn't have been the only ones. Last year I had the joy of observing a man in Philadelphia who was the opposite of a weekend zombie. In fact, he did his job with so much passion that I would call him a "Life Poet." He sang and danced as he emptied trash cans into the truck.

Bring passion to whatever you do. Consider masons building a brick wall. If you ask, "What are you doing?" one may answer, "Can't you see I'm stacking bricks to make a wall?" A second mason at the same jobsite may tell you, "I'm here making the most beautiful building in the whole city." They're talking about the same work, but the second worker visualizes the end result and takes pride in it. Like him—and the trash collector—you too can join the army of Life Poets if you can find the passion in your work.

HOW TO FIND OR RECOVER YOUR PASSION

When I ask people about their passion or purpose, they often don't have a clue. If you're in that category, ask yourself a variation on the question that led to Warren Buffett's advice: "What would I do if money were not an issue or if every job on the planet received equal pay?" These questions apply because many people tell me they can't follow their passion "because nobody pays for that." Another question also applies: "What would I do even if I weren't going to be paid for it?"

Alice Barker would have danced. In a video shot in her hospital room,[2] the 102-year-old former dancer lay motionless until visitors showed movies of her in a Harlem chorus line in the 1940s. Hearing the music and seeing herself dance clearly energized and delighted the lady. Then she said, "I used to often say to myself, 'I'm being paid to do something that I enjoy doing, and I would do it for free.'" Watching her dance with passion—more than any of the other dancers in the group—you can be certain she meant it.

DOING THINGS TO PLEASE OTHERS INSTEAD OF OURSELVES

Many of us end up doing things we don't love to make other people happy or to keep from making them *un*happy. This often occurs because we're conditioned from an early age to feel responsible for other people's feelings. For example, a mother might tell her child, "I'm unhappy because you didn't clean your room. *You* made me unhappy."

That conditioning endures. I know plenty of people in their fifties and sixties who won't let themselves live the

---

[2] http://alicebarkernotbaker.com/2016.

lives they want. One sixty-eight-year-old woman I know smokes cigarettes, but her ninety-year-old parents don't know it because she has never felt free enough to tell them.

Now, I don't smoke or even like smoking, and it's useful to acknowledge that we're social beings who can and do affect others' feelings. But the example of the ashamed smoker illustrates how people voluntarily let the opinions of others control how they live their own lives. They often have a mental image of the way to be perfect for other people but no image of how to be perfect for themselves. They must remember to live their own lives.

Another way people commonly thwart their passion in the interest of others is by desiring to impress someone. In fact, it's so common that it's part of this popular quote: "Many people buy things they don't need with money they don't have to impress people they don't like."[3]

What can you do about these *self*-sacrifices? You might consider yourself the director of the movie of your life. Who's the hero in your movie? Your kids? Your parents? Your mate? It should be *you*.

When I propose that experiment and ask that question in my seminars, many participants point to someone else—never to themselves. That common choice makes

---

3   Unknown source. https://quoteinvestigator.com/tag/walter-slezak/.

them responsible for the feelings of the person or people they place in the starring role.

When I ask the participants to make *themselves* the hero of their own lives instead, I often hear reactions like, "How selfish! It's all about me, me, me!" I have to remind them that it's *their* life. It's not only all about them, but they (you) should come first in their (your) story. You need to reach your potential before you can help others fully reach theirs.

CHANGE YOUR APPROACH

If even thinking about making yourself happy continues to challenge you, begin by focusing on what you love doing. For example, if you love having candlelight dinners, visualize all the details and the senses of that dinner—the location, the room, the tastes, the smells, and the look of the food. While you visualize this lovely experience, you're retraining your brain to think about what you want, and not what you don't. If you've already been visualizing what you want, do it more often.

A related brain-retraining suggestion is to list the things you love doing. List as many as fifty or even a hundred activities, even those you haven't done in years. *Your* list might include activities like skiing, walking in the park, chatting with friends, going to the theater, dancing, and singing in the shower when nobody's listening. Anything

YOU NEED TO REACH
YOUR POTENTIAL BEFORE
YOU CAN HELP OTHERS
FULLY REACH THEIRS.

goes because the exercise is only redirecting your brain to where you want to be; it's not a to-do list.

List these beloved activities as they occur to you, and don't rank them. For the purpose of brain retraining, priority doesn't matter. Keep the list handy, add to it over time, and reread it frequently.

HOW ELSE PASSION LINKS TO PURPOSE

As you continue to focus on what you love to do, that focus will eventually give you a window into your passion. Your purpose, then, is how you apply that passion to your daily life. What you love to do can and will guide you to something bigger. For example, when I was in elementary and middle school, I was always the class clown. I loved to be in front of the class and to entertain my classmates and teachers. Later on, as a teenager with the same affinity, I became the lead singer and guitar player in a rock band.

With that background, however long ago, it's no coincidence that I've since found my passion and purpose in inspiring and teaching people as a trainer, speaker, and teacher. I've found a way to make people happy that fulfills me more than singing ever did. As a singer, I would probably have had to sing about broken hearts, unrequited love, and other effects of limiting beliefs. I believe that unhappiness is a choice, though, not a mandate. I would never glorify it, in song or anywhere else.

THREE PASSION KILLERS

As you're identifying your passion in pursuit of happiness, beware of the three most common ways people sabotage their progress.

1. Fear

One of the biggest obstacles to finding one's passion is fear. Although people are often aware of that fear, they often can't identify its source. It's too abstract.

If one of my clients had allowed it, her mother's fear might've derailed her plans to earn a living making marionettes. Her mother insisted, "You can't earn a living from puppets! You're a doctor!" My client didn't take on the fear, though; she followed her passion, and her puppets are a huge success. It's no coincidence that she branded them "Puppets That Heal the Soul™."

Push back against people who tell you that you cannot live on your passion. Don't be so quick to believe them or even yourself. You also might search for people who already do for a living what you're passionate about. If you find any other practitioners of your passion, you'll know you can do it too. If you don't, you probably didn't look closely enough. But if you exhaust the possibilities without finding anyone, that's probably also good news. It might mean you've discovered a new market for yourself.

2. Ease

Magnetizing makes change easy, and the ease itself can block progress. What do I mean by that? Most of us value only things that are *hard*, so we can view things that come too easily to us as worthless. This is because of the conditioned ideal of struggle we receive from our parents, teachers, and most of the world, including literature and movies. The hero struggles in almost every single movie; the greater the struggle, the greater the reward at the end.

The relative perceived value of ease versus struggle is like the difference between getting something for free and buying something with money we worked hard to earn.

This story demonstrates the strength of the ease obstacle. One client came to my twelve-day seminar for help in overcoming his social phobia. He even feared being stopped on the street by someone asking the time. His fear of people was so powerful, in fact, that he almost decided not to walk into the seminar room on the first day. He was also the only person I've ever met who didn't know how to laugh, or even smile.

In less than two hours, my partner and I taught him how to smile, laugh, and be confident, using a simple technique. Because it was simple, though, he didn't recognize or trust his dramatic progress. To help him appreciate the change, I asked, "Would your father be prouder of you if you said making something beautiful was hard or easy?" "Hard," he said instantly. I pointed out that he couldn't change his father's perspective but that he needed to change his own. He needed to learn to acknowledge and respect achievements that come easily. He did.[4]

3. Perceived Difficulty

On the other side of the coin, we may not even start to explore a potential passion because we perceive it to be hard. For example, learning math or languages has that common perception. Instead of letting it stop you, again change your approach. Ask yourself how you can make it easier for yourself. Instead of dreading a struggle when you take on your goal, how can you imagine yourself dancing through it, like the Philadelphia trash collector?

GIVING YOURSELF CREDIT FOR EVERY SUCCESS

Another way to retrain your brain, reinforce your growth,

---

[4] When I ran into my client at a restaurant two years after that seminar, he was a different person. Seated at an outside table by a lake, he was animated, chatting, and laughing with a beautiful woman who hung on his every word.

and dance through challenges is to practice patting yourself on the back for everything you can. Frequent positive feedback helps you stay focused on your progress. That idea may be as new to you as it was for my formerly agoraphobic client. When I suggested it, he asked, "If I take credit, doesn't that stop the process?" He so feared self-praise that he hadn't ever given himself credit for *anything*. He had to learn that adopting the habit was in fact helpful, not the opposite.

I had to learn it too. Years ago, I was my own worst enemy. For example, if I dropped a knife in the kitchen, I'd criticize myself: "I'm so useless that I can't even hold a knife!" These days, though, I'm more likely to praise myself for how brilliantly I pick up a dropped knife. I'll go so far as to congratulate myself for being a genius, saying that no one in the world can pick up a knife as well as I can! I've developed the habit of giving myself credit for things large and small.

Give yourself credit even if your success came easily and even if the act of taking credit feels fake. It's still another case of faking it until you make it and reprogramming your brain. Praising yourself for everything also reminds you to be your own best friend—the hero in your life. Deactivate the belief that saying nice things to yourself is egotistical. It isn't; it's encouraging.

In Slovakia, it's common to feel it's wrong to praise oneself. In fact, there's even a popular saying that, in effect, self-praise stinks. I never heard my parents speak well of themselves. No one ever *punished* me if I said something positive about myself, but no one ever *encouraged* me to do it, either. Instead, self-criticism—by parents, by teachers, by peers, and in movies—was the norm in my environment.

THE RED THREAD

After you free yourself from all this bullshit, you'll be better equipped to find the "red thread," which is the trail back to your roots and toward your passion. The red thread helps you answer your life's essential questions, including, "When I strip away my limiting beliefs, what do I really love?" and the biggest one, "Why am I here?" Following the red thread as far back as necessary can point out your passions and clear even a dusty trail.

The goal of following the thread—and, in fact, the purpose of this book—is to help you remember who you really are. It's not to teach anything new about yourself. To help yourself remember, write down anything in your childhood that you did with passion. That includes things like every game, every trip with your parents, any favorite school subject, any hobby, and any fondly remembered activity with your friends.

Also, recall and list anything that was easy for you. For

example, maybe you could easily learn the words to songs or poems, or maybe you excelled at sports. Maybe you were good at telling stories or listening. Remember how it felt to do these things so you can recover and relive that joyful feeling. Then ask yourself how you can bring it into your adult life.

I wish my father had known how. One rainy Sunday, when I was about ten years old, I asked him to play a game with me. Although we had played together many times before, this day was to be different. He responded, "I'm an adult now. I'm not good at playing." Despite earlier proof to the contrary, I turned this shocking statement into a belief that adults could not be playful.

Then and there, I promised myself that *I* would never stop playing. I forgot that promise until years later, when my mentor suggested I recover my playfulness and apply it to my work. If you loved playing as a child, I advise you to do the same, whatever your job, including parenting.

IN AND OUT OF THE FOREST

I like the image of the red thread because it's reminiscent of fairy tales old and new. The title and tale of *The Red Thread: An Adoption Fairy Tale*, by Grace Lin, refers to the invisible thread believed by ancient Chinese people to link those who belong together. In "Hansel and Gretel," the children drop breadcrumbs in the hopes of finding their way out of the dark forest. I'm asking you to imagine the red thread that connects from your childhood to your present day. It's there to help lead you out of the forest and back to your passions.

I'll say it again: It's not only okay to find and embrace your passion. It's actually *essential* because that's where the most energy, influence, and joy lie. Our beautiful planet already contains enough weekend zombies. We need more Life Poets who, in embracing their passions, inspire us and make the world a better place.

So, magnetize your passions—harness that energy that pulls you toward your dreams. Now that you know what to do and how to do it, I ask you to imagine this scenario: If I gave you access to a time machine that would show you your future, would you step into it? If you would, please fasten your seat belt because in the next chapter, *you'll visit your future*.

MAGIC QUESTIONS

- When you strip away your limiting beliefs, what do you really love?
- What would you do if money were not an issue or if every job on the planet received equal pay?
- What would you want to do even if you weren't going to be paid for it?

- How can you imagine yourself dancing through your job, like the Philadelphia trash collector?
- What are the consequences of not following your passion?
- Also ask the biggest question: Why are you here?

CHAPTER 3

A—ALL SENSES: YOUR TIME MACHINE

YOUR FUTURE IS WAITING for you to create it. Can you *sense* it?

By this point in the book, you've learned to use clarity and magnetism to figure out and express what you want and why you want it. You've also learned that to gain the support of your subconscious, it's important to express your future in the precise language it understands. That language consists of more than words, even precise ones. When you talk to your subconscious, you need to show, not tell.

To create the future you dream of, *visualize* your goals. As you're about to learn, visualization includes more than just the visual sense. When you rely on only one sense, it's as if you limit your car to one gear when you want to go full speed. This chapter's mission is to show you how to use all your senses to create your future in a precise way. They're the time machine that will whisk you there.

PLAYING FAVORITES

Most people favor one sense, which means they use it more often or intensely than the other senses. Recognizing your favored sense will remind you to engage the others. That's one of the two reasons that, when I work with clients, I begin by identifying which sense is most important to them.[1]

People aren't necessarily aware of their strongest sense. For example, top athletes often assume they favor the kinesthetic sense because they perform with their body. Yet the kinesthetic sense is often athletes' *secondary* sense. It's their *visual* strategies that mainly drive their success.

For most people of all descriptions, the three primary senses are seeing (visual), hearing (auditory), and touching (kinesthetic). Visual, the most common, is often the only one people use to visualize their future. Again, though, favoring one sense represents only a portion of your capabilities.

---

[1] The other reason I identify clients' primary sense is to help us bond. You might also find this technique useful in your own relationships. Mirroring senses helps people feel understood and connected. For example, kinesthetic people want to touch their problems and to connect with one another. They respond to literal touch as well as words that evoke connecting, touching, and feeling.

In my experience, people rarely favor the sense of smell (olfactory), but it's also powerful. When people in this sensory group tap into memories, smells influence what they see and hear. A client who sells to retail stores asked for help in recalling the stores' names, a task that most people would achieve by drawing on their visual or auditory sense. Because the sales rep favors the olfactory sense, though, she met her goal by associating each store with a particular smell.

If you haven't yet achieved some of *your* goals, though, it's more likely that you're not using enough of your senses rather than misreading or underutilizing your strongest one. Focusing on one sense cheats you of the power of integrated senses in your visualizations.

SENSING YOUR FUTURE FROM THE OUTCOME IN

The good news is that you already know how to visualize with all of your senses. That's true even if you aren't aware of it and even if you don't use the process to consciously create your future. Your senses are already contributing to your beliefs about your reality.

For example, if I were to ask how you know your car *is* in fact your car, you're likely to show me your bill of sale. You're less likely to respond with senses-based reasons, although they are the truest. For example, they might enable you to describe what you experienced in the vehicle. Or you might describe how it looks, feels, or smells or how it sounds when you start the engine. Maybe you remember the material and the position of your seats or what was in the glove box. You can recall many details.

That's the same sensory language I suggest you use to build scenarios that help you "remember" your future.

Engage that sensory language to help your subconscious lead you to the future you dream of by imagining how your life will change after, and as a result of, achieving your dream. For example, Maria Sharapova reported in a media interview that she visualizes her future to help her win world-class tennis tournaments.

In addition to imagining specific, single goals, like winning a grand slam, Sharapova considers how that win would change her life and how she would feel about those changes. Like all successful athletes, she starts by seeing herself taking the gold, not silver or bronze.

To be a champion, visualize like one. Lowered expectations bring lesser results. For some people, if they make it to a tournament or some other event, they hope only that they don't embarrass themselves. What a waste of potential!

You don't need to be an athlete to benefit from visualizing your future as a champion. To support my dream of success as an author, I use multiple senses to visualize readers thanking me by email or in person on the street. I see and hear them, feel their handshakes and hugs, and feel the sun on my face.

To round out the image, I imagine smelling various colognes and coffees. Sometimes I even engage my sense of taste by imagining sipping my favorite warm beverage as people greet me. This technique works for me, and if you use it, it will also work for you.

INSTALLING FEELINGS IN YOUR SCENARIO

If you notice where particular feelings live in your body, you often can engage them when you want to. For example, consider retiring athletes who get stuck in the transition to the business world because they fail to use the subconscious strategies that brought them success as an athlete.

When I work with former athletes, I often ask them to recall a situation in which they felt confident and excelled. I help them analyze that feeling—how it feels, what size and shape it is, and where it lives in the body.

Being asked to describe the feeling helps the former athletes, and anyone else, to recognize those feelings. If we've installed the strategy properly, former athletes will start to experience confidence in their new careers as they did when they were successful in the past.

WAKE UP

Before you can install feelings, you need to be able to identify them. Even some of the world's greatest athletes aren't aware of their subconscious strategies; they haven't linked them to their conscious minds. Consider the professional golfer I worked with who visualized his swings. Stating a goal to have more good days than bad ones, he said he couldn't control that outcome.

When I asked him to describe his best hits, he trotted out his standard answers about the ball's trajectory, the way it hit the green, and the direction of the wind. He was already visualizing, but mostly with his visual sense. This time, though, my question helped him be aware of his actual method. He subconsciously judged the hit's quality by the sound of the club against the ball.

To encourage good hits, we worked on making him aware of what he had been sensing only subconsciously: the sweet sound of a perfect hit as he swung the club. This method was worth a million dollars to this golfer. By adding the sense of sound to his visualization, his best shots no longer felt as random.

When I recommend to clients that they add sound to their visualizations, they often ask me to supply a recording of the appropriate one. People tend to seek and trust outside resources. But as the golfer discovered, your brain is the best recorder. When you're in the activity, you can draw on only what you have in your head. It's not practical to plan on carrying around and using an audio recorder. You have everything you need inside you. Using the techniques in this book will help you practice to the point that you'll begin to engage more senses in every visualization.

LET YOUR SUBCONSCIOUS PROPEL YOU FORWARD

In college, I dreamed of playing on the university's hockey team, and I practiced sensory visualization long before I was aware of its value. I knew only that I loved thinking about hockey, not that doing so was programming me for success.

Hockey stick in hand even when I rode the subway, I would visualize myself on the ice. When I looked down, I could see my skates and the ice below me. I could hear the distinctive sounds of the rink and feel the exhilaration of being there. I could smell it, maybe the easiest sense to call up under the circumstances. Hockey *stinks*. I don't know of any type of locker room in the world that smells worse than the one at an ice-hockey rink. (Hockey players, though, love this smell!)

I credit my sensory visualization, not only my hours of physical practice, with my success at making the team despite being thirty years old, at least ten years older than my teammates. In visualizing myself making good passes, winning pucks, and skating well, I created my future.

Of course, I wasn't aware I was visualizing. If I had been, I would also have visualized scoring goals. I'm sure I would have scored more, especially if I had experienced in my mind the sights, sounds, smells, feelings, and maybe even the tastes of scoring.

THE "SECRET" LANGUAGE OF THE SUBCONSCIOUS

I'm calling subconscious language "secret" (with quotes) because although you already speak it—as often as thousands of times each day—you may not be aware you do. To become more aware that you speak it, imagine switching on a light in your kitchen. Because you've performed the action so many times, you can also perform it in your mind, in vivid sensory detail. I'm asking you to use that language to put your subconscious to work on creating your desired future.

If you want to, say, be a better tennis player, consider this: Hitting a tennis ball perfectly is no more difficult than turning on a light switch. If you're not as good at hitting the ball as you are at working the switch, it's because tennis's unlimited possibilities for methods and outcomes—including the uncontrollable performance of the opponent—can trigger limiting beliefs.

In tennis, the main reason people improve with practice is that they change the way they think about playing. I've seen players whose solo practice helps them hit a soda can a thousand times to the same spot. Put them up without practice or visualization against an opponent, though, and they're lost.

If you have children, you can distinguish their voices from anyone else's. You can even precisely imagine them. You have the same abilities with every sense. Like using muscles, precisely speaking the sensory language of the subconscious gets better with practice.

Awareness of the language of the subconscious doesn't mean you'll be the next Maria Sharapova or Bill Gates.[2] It will help you, though, to quickly achieve the outcomes you desire. Think of the language of the subconscious as a computer-programming language. You have the ability to reprogram your subconscious to success and happiness.

---

[2] It also doesn't exclude the possibility!

DREAM IN COLOR AND MORE

Visualizing with all your senses, not just the visual, makes even the visual stronger and more concrete. In addition, I encourage you to explore the many qualities within each sense. The many possible visual qualities include the following:

- Are there any colors in your visualization? If so, how many are there? What are they? How intense are they? Instead, is the picture black and white or gray? Color or not, how much contrast is there?
- What's the size, shape, and dimension of the visualization?
- How close or distant is the picture you see?
- What's its resolution? Is it in sharp focus or blurry?
- Is the picture still or moving?

To supply your subconscious with everything it needs to support your dream, include vivid, moving detail.[3] Moving pictures, in particular, go far to mirror reality, so they can add an emotional intensity that helps you *feel* your future. If you're an athlete dreaming of scoring more goals, visualize big, intense, and detailed three-dimensional moving pictures.

---

[3] The only place I recommend that you don't think in vivid, big pictures is when you're working on your phobias. There I would use the opposite strategy—visualizations that are small, in the distance, and without motion. To find out exactly how to lose a phobia, you might consider taking my course in it.

Other senses bring countless variations as well. Consider sounds, for example. Where do they come from? Are they close or distant? What's the volume? Are they harmonious or discordant? Are they made of voices, music, nature, machines, or something else? How many and whose voices are there? Do you recognize the music? If you include self-talk, what does it sound—and feel—like when you say positive or negative things to yourself?

GIVING YOUR SUBCONSCIOUS A BOOST

Respect the uniqueness of each scenario and build it from scratch. Although your mind can build the ideal scenario without adding data from reality, you might find it helpful to inject a dose of the real world. For example, when I plan a speaking engagement, I show up at the venue at least a day before the event so I can see the room.

Going through every sense that applies, I mentally note the room's size, colors, and furnishings to set the scene for my visualization of a successful gig. I visualize a standing ovation in that room, with people approaching me afterward to ask questions and buy my books.

I connect with the audience members before I even meet them by visualizing the presentation itself, including the look, sound, and feel of an engaged audience. I also picture the experience of having some audience members who lose their concentration, so I'm prepared to respond constructively rather than panic.

During these sorts of visualizations, I don't necessarily picture every face in the crowd, but I do see faces. I want to be able to read expressions, so I can read the level of engagement.

Judge the quality of your visualizations not by whether they're good or bad, but by their ability to support your desired future. Contrast my visualizations before a presentation with those of people who are terrified of public speaking. They do visualize, but what *they* imagine before I help them are the senses associated with an unfriendly, bored, confused, or even hostile audience.

Those examples demonstrate that you make your reality, and if you want a different one, you have to change something. Although those people put in the same amount of content preparation as I do, they're likely to fail because they're not properly preparing their visualizations.

As another example, if you dream of a new house, use all of your senses to paint a precise picture of the one you want. See it up close with your dear ones living in it; maybe picture yourself walking in the front door. See and feel all the details on your way in; smell the flowers in the yard. Hear the front door opening, your feet on the floor, and the ceiling fan.

As you look around further, do you hear music? What other sounds do you hear, or is it quiet? Does someone welcome you? Touch the walls and the floors. What texture and temperature are they? How does it feel inside the house? Did you take your shoes off in the garden and dip your feet into the pool? What else is in the pool? Are there people, rafts, rubber ducks, bugs, or leaves?

The more sensory details the better—they help you "remember your future." That's so much more useful to the subconscious than just saying, "I want a nice house."

Real estate listing agents also know the value of sensory details in installing powerful visualizations. To help prospects see themselves living in a listed house, they commonly tell their clients to bake something with an inviting aroma, like cookies or bread.

SENSORY NEGOTIATING

Let's examine the scenario of asking for a raise and see how the senses can help. When you visualize the encounter, start with the end state. To open a space for your imagination, ask yourself how you'll know if the negotiations went well. Fill that space with all the sensory pictures that implant that positive outcome. Imagine your supervisor's welcoming smile and body language, the receptive sound of her voice praising your work, the smell of her coffee or perfume, the celebratory taste of your coffee, and the feel of the handshake that seals the deal.

Imagining that perfect world should always be your first step. You might also find it wise to prepare your *conscious* mind to respond to any objections. Never start there, though. Never plant the idea of any sort of failure in your subconscious.

Positive visualizations, even multisensory ones, won't work every time, but they will increase your success rate. When they don't work, improve future outcomes by examining what might have gone wrong in your visualization process.

In the rare cases when you don't succeed despite a well-informed subconscious, look for other probable causes. For example, these might include taking on someone else's dream for you instead of your own. They might also include failing to follow your visualization with sufficient conscious preparation or real actions, which you'll explore in the next chapter.

MESSY THOUGHTS

Despite its popularity, worrying is one strategy that never helps. It's messy. Think of those people you met earlier in this chapter who sabotage their presentations by expecting the worst. If you're a worrywart, I urge you to stop because your worrying is *creating* your future, and a worrisome one at that. Fear the worst, and you're likely to get it.

You can see this behavior express itself in statements like "Everything I look forward to always ends in catastrophe." If that reflects your own thoughts, you can blame your attitude for the outcome. Before you can create effective visualizations, you'll need to change your beliefs. Believing that you're responsible for creating your reality is a good start.

Worrying affects your body language, which in turn affects your behavior and that of others. You both feel and express it with most of your senses. For example, what happens if you bring body language that reflects worry about a negative outcome into a meeting with your CEO? You're likely to radiate the aspects—the look, feel, sound, and maybe even the smell—of prey. You'll give the CEO little choice but to unconsciously respond in a predator-like fashion.

But if you instead show up as an equal, the CEO will register that and respond to your show of confidence.

A CASE IN POINT

As a further example of the prey-predator relationship, one of my clients has a father who dominated her. Even though she's an adult and a parent herself, she feared every encounter with him. I asked her to begin to change that reality by recalling, with all her senses, what was different about the body language of people whom he considered his equals.

Then I asked her to show me her typical behavior when she visited her father in his office. She tapped on the door, opened it a crack, and, in a timid voice, asked, "May I?" The second act in the visualization role-play was to imagine entering the office with confidence. She was to knock soundly, open the door as though she meant it, kiss her father on the cheek, tell him, "When you have a chance, I want to speak with you," and walk out.

At first she refused, saying she could never even *imagine* doing that. Eventually, though, she not only imagined it—she *did* it. She reported that her new manner surprised and impressed her father. It also earned her a hug and her first-ever deep conversation with him.

FOCUS ON THE OUTCOME

At this stage, it's more important to focus on and visualize the outcome than to focus on the process.

How often and for how long should you visualize each outcome? There's no right or wrong answer. You might follow Maria Sharapova's lead. She said she often visualizes the end state, and she does it spontaneously. She never forces it. If you're new to visualization, though, you might state an intention—maybe to visualize before meals and bedtime and when you wake up.

Visualizing should be easy to fit in if you make it a game. It is fun to imagine traveling in a time machine. In addition, the fact that you're imagining a desired future with all of your senses should generate good feelings and inspire you to repeat the practice often.

MAGIC QUESTIONS

Recall a time when you easily achieved a goal.

- Before you achieved it, did you visualize a positive outcome?
- Did you visualize it in vivid sensory detail?
- What were the details? Recall the sights, sounds, smells, feelings, and tastes you associated with it.

Now recall a time when you didn't achieve a goal you set.

- Instead of visualizing a positive outcome, did you get stuck in planning a process?

- If you didn't get stuck in the process, is it possible you visualized with only one sense and not with your full range?

PRACTICE ON YOUR OWN

As an exercise, practice visualizing a positive outcome you desire. Start with the outcome, be concrete, use all your senses, and make the pictures big, three-dimensional, and colorful. It's easy.

Now that you've visited your future through your senses, it's time to set your course. What you need now is your map to guide you so you don't lose your way. You'll get that map in the next chapter.

CHAPTER 4

G–GPS: THE MAP TO THE LIFE YOU WANT

HOW DO YOU KNOW if you're getting close to achieving your dream? You're working so hard. You're following the advice in other books about meeting goals. So why aren't you there yet?

You're either not reading or not *heeding* the continuous feedback life sends you.

Feedback is your Global Positioning System (GPS). It's your map. The GPS model shows you whether you're heading toward your goal and where you are in relation to it. Feedback is also like road signs, though not nearly as clearly marked, so watch for it with all your senses. When you do, if you don't like the feedback you're getting, you have several choices: You can drive through or around roadblocks, take a detour, change your direction, or change your destination.

HOW TO KNOW WHETHER YOU'RE COMING OR GOING

Maybe you took the right steps to achieve your goals, but you didn't notice that you were actually heading in the *wrong* direction. The faster you ran, the farther away you ultimately found yourself from where you wanted to be. Maybe you also got stuck in the steps.

Following the wrong path is such a waste of time and source of frustration that no one would do it consciously. Why, then, does it happen so often? It happens because the traveler fails to deliberately stop at various points along the way to check the GPS and evaluate progress. Feedback—there for the taking—is there to guide you if you'll only stop and listen.

Take this simple example. Let's say you need to go from Chicago to Washington, DC, so you hop into the car and onto the highway. Your car has no GPS, and you left your house without a map. How would you recognize that you're on the right road? Of course, you would follow the road signs: Washington...Washington...Washington...

What would you do if instead of signs for Washington,

you saw signs that show you're heading in a totally wrong direction? Los Angeles...Los Angeles...Los Angeles... what would you do? It's likely you'd stop to ask and then change directions.

Although that behavior is intuitive on a literal road, most people don't behave that way on their life's path. Without receiving training in analyzing situations, they often react to the feedback that suggests the wrong direction by working harder and investing more effort. Their tenacity is admirable, but with every step, they're moving further from their goal. It's like driving faster when you're going the wrong way on a highway. It makes no sense!

A LABYRINTH, NOT A STEPLADDER

People often lose direction because they insist on planning every step. Let's look at a few more examples to help show why you need a GPS, set to your desired outcome, to guide you. Contrary to popular belief, the pursuit of goals (and life itself!) is like a labyrinth in which people can and often do get lost. The process is rarely a neat step-by-step path like a ladder leading you by linear rungs toward or away your goals.

People often get lost and frustrated because they plan—and get attached to—every step. When uncontrollable circumstances change, as they almost always do, steps need to change with them. Instead, those well-intentioned but misguided planners get stuck in steps that no longer support the outcome. These people can sabotage their success.

Consider a consultant whose process dictates certain required steps for attracting new business clients. Steps include sending emails, calling CEOs' assistants, and requesting meetings. If, say, the assistants fail to cooperate, the stuck consultant is more likely to repeat steps that aren't working or give up than to be creative.

Paying attention to your GPS as part of the M.A.G.I.C. model will keep you flexible enough to respond to change. I cannot imagine a chess master who would plan every move before a match instead of staying flexible enough to react to what's happening right now. The model's flexibility represents a stark and welcome contrast to the outdated model of the world that focused on fighting and manipulating people and environments.

LET YOUR VALUES GUIDE YOU

People can lose direction on their goals because they haven't figured out what their goals are really about. You need to deeply understand the principle of "the goal behind the goal." Goals are always about more than they appear to be. Your GPS, programmed with your values, will help you get to the bottom of your goals.

You may already appreciate the importance of value-based goals if you've ever reached a coveted goal only to discover that attaining it didn't make you happy. True fulfillment comes not from reaching the goals but from experiencing your values during your journey to get there.[1]

Let's say your goal is your dream house. You will have a better chance of reaching this goal if you understand the values connected to owning the house. Maybe you associate it with security and love. (Goals may have more than one associated value.) You can program your GPS with those values. Then, when your GPS shows you the "Security" and "Love" signs, you'll know you're on the right track.

If instead the signs read "Frustration," "Fear," or "Struggle," your GPS is trying to tell you that you're heading in the wrong direction, so pay attention and turn around. It's worth repeating that you don't have to struggle to reach your goals, even though you may think you do. (Of course, if frustration, fear, or struggle *is* your value, don't change a thing!)

---

[1] However, you may be thinking, "So does that mean that the journey is the goal? Goals don't make us happy, so I should get rid of them to be only in the present moment?" Not exactly. If you're focused on the here and now without any destination, a journey doesn't make sense. The Chinese people have a saying that applies: "If you don't know where you're heading, it doesn't matter which path you take."

TRUE FULFILLMENT COMES NOT FROM REACHING THE GOALS BUT FROM EXPERIENCING YOUR VALUES DURING YOUR JOURNEY TO GET THERE.

THE VALUES-FEELINGS LINK

You want your goals for deeper reasons than just the goals themselves. If your goal is buying that dream house, again, you want it for what's behind the goal—what the house represents. Your GPS will be even more precise if you program it with your feelings as well as your values.

As more confirmation that goals are about more than they seem, let's revisit the dream house. If acquiring the house were *your* dream, I would start by asking you why you want that particular house and what it represents to you. I would ask you to consider what part of your life would improve if you owned the house. I would ask what you want to feel in that house.

I ask those questions in my seminars, and people often respond that it will make them feel more secure. I follow up by asking why security is important to them, and I may hear that it makes them feel productive—that's another value uncovered. The goal then is about the values of security and productivity.

Then I dive into each answer, asking why security is important to them and what it feels like when they imagine being secure. Each question leads to another connection, and I ask attendees to list each one. By the time we finish, they've listed four or six words that represent their core values—their road signs to look for to show they're on the right path.

Every time a client expresses *any* dream, I ask these two questions:

- Why is your desired outcome important to you?
- How will reaching that outcome improve your life?

For example, feelings and values may guide you well on your choice of a life partner. Let's say you have a specific one in mind. When you ask yourself what you want to experience with that person, you can look for feedback to reinforce your choice. It could be a feeling of happiness that you associate with that person, or you might share values, such as a devotion to a particular religion or lifestyle.[2]

Going through that process on your own or with me will highlight your values and encourage you to incorporate them in your life now. Don't defer it.

VALUES ORIENT PERCEPTION

Another reason to identify your values is that your per-

---

[2] In case you're wondering, though, not even M.A.G.I.C. can guarantee that the person you choose will also choose you. That person has their own collection of values, feelings, senses, and goals that may run counter to yours.

ceptions and expectations create your reality and your path to it, as the shopkeeper story illustrates.

A newcomer to the city entered a shop and approached the shopkeeper with a question: "Can you tell me what kind of people live in this city?" The wise proprietor responded by asking the man to describe his former townspeople.

The customer said he hated them because they're jealous and dishonest; he complained that thieves had broken into his apartment three times. The shopkeeper had bad news for him: "The same kind of people live here too."

A few days later, a different newcomer came to the shop with the identical question. When the shopkeeper responded with *his* same question, the newcomer described his former neighbors as helpful and friendly and expressed his sadness that he had to leave them. At this, the shopkeeper smiled and said he didn't need to be sad because "the same kind of people live *here too*."

Vastly different paths to the same place led two people to opposite realities. As you cannot expect to reach Washington if you follow signs to LA, you cannot expect to be happy, productive, and secure by following the path to frustration.

VALUES ALSO GUIDE BEHAVIOR

When you connect with your values, they can guide your behavior to align with those values. For my first book, I commissioned a designer. On the appointed delivery date—carefully chosen to support the book's projected release schedule, I found that he had not even begun the work.

I'm human, so I was angry. I could have expressed that anger by yelling at him and demanding that he keep his promise. I could have *sued* him. Instead, though, I knew to connect with my book's values: inspiring and encouraging change. I realized that I could not pour negative energy into my book. So I thanked him and turned for help to a friend who referred me to a compatible designer. This one treated me like a valued customer and completed the beautiful design quickly and collaboratively.

The experience validates the GPS model. If I had chosen to struggle, I would have failed to produce the book and the energy I wanted in my life. In that case, then, I believe the book would have drawn a different type of person to my seminars. Because I stayed positive throughout, I had the experience and the outcome I dreamed of.

The experience also reinforces the fallacy of insisting on planning every step. I could not have planned on connecting with that designer of my dreams; he didn't return from travel until the day before I knew I would need him to replace the other one.

Compare that reality to a client's friend who, like the guy who saw himself as unlucky in the TV show, expects bad outcomes because he has a history of them. In his mind, bad outcomes drown out any good ones. For him, machines always seem to stop working, and in restaurants, his food is always served cold. He has run into a person on a motorcycle with his car; it turned out he didn't hurt her, but he assumed he had. He has also been *kidnapped.*

Using my seminar's techniques, my client helped her friend change his life.[3] He discovered that the more he fought his life's circumstances instead of flowing with them, the more things worked against him.

CHOOSE HAPPINESS NOW

As the wise proverb goes, "You cannot have a happy ending to an unhappy journey."[4] Instead of trying to force the process of working toward your dreams, consider how you can enjoy it. It's fun to imagine an outcome, especially a positive one, with all your senses. What's more important is that choosing happiness is more likely than

---

3   When you go deeper into these principles at my seminars, you can also help your friends and family members change their lives.

4   From Abraham-Hicks Publications.

struggle and pressure to lead you to your destination, as talent shows like *America's Got Talent* illustrate.

You can often predict winners by hearing the performers speak in backstage interviews. Some focus on the opportunity as the only chance to change their life. Those performers tend to put pressure on themselves that interferes with their ability to connect with the judges and the audience. They're not reading their GPS. They rarely even make it to the next round.

By contrast, the winners tend to come in happy and take it easy. They often express desires to inspire people or to do their best. They're able to let go.[5]

How about you? What would happen if you didn't achieve your dreams? Do you quickly answer, "This would be terrible?" If you really think about it, though, you'll realize that nothing bad would happen.

That thinking is useful because it takes away the importance of the outcome, so you can feel less attached to it. Achieving or even losing your dreams should never be attached to desperate feelings. In fact, feeing less attached even helps you achieve your full potential.

At this point, then, if your GPS is delivering feedback

---

[5] In German, letting go is known as *los lassen* or "The LoLa Principle."

ACHIEVING OR EVEN LOSING YOUR DREAMS SHOULD NEVER BE ATTACHED TO DESPERATE FEELINGS.

you don't like, think about what you need to change. For example, financial security is a common goal among my seminar participants. When I recommend that they practice feeling wealthy, some of them look at me as though I'm crazy. When they insist that their bank accounts can't support that feeling, I'm ready with an answer.

I suggest they look at areas of abundance that their lives already contain—their beloved family members and friends, as well as natural blessings like air, water, and food. To feel happy or healthy now if you don't, look to times in your life when you did feel them. And, as you learned in the previous chapters, use your senses and positive words to visualize your goals. Make your journey happy and make it support your values *now*, rather than in some distant future after you reach your destination.

We'll leave this chapter with a well-timed caveat: No GPS in the world can tell you what you want. The tool requires you to set the destination first.

Have you set your destination yet? Great! Now you've got your map. You're about to get on the road.

MAGIC QUESTIONS
- What do you want your life to look like?
- How will you feel at your destination?

MAKE YOUR JOURNEY HAPPY AND MAKE IT SUPPORT YOUR VALUES NOW, RATHER THAN IN SOME DISTANT FUTURE AFTER YOU REACH YOUR DESTINATION.

- Why are your goals important to you?
- Why are the values behind those goals important to you?
- How will reaching those goals improve your life?
- What will you experience more of in your life when you achieve your goals?

CHAPTER 5

I–INSPIRED ACTION: THE VEHICLE THAT TAKES YOU TO YOUR FUTURE LIFE

ONCE YOU BRING CLARITY to your dreams, magnetize purpose, and listen to your GPS, strange but wonderful things are likely to show up in your life. Don't be surprised if you find yourself with new business offers and more choices. That's the signal that the Wave has worked. You're ready to move beyond visualizing your goal. It's time to take inspired action[1]—the next M.A.G.I.C. step.

---

[1] The term "inspired action" came from Abraham Hicks, a spiritual being who speaks through Esther Hicks, who, with her husband Jerry Hicks, writes and presents seminars on spiritual topics. Rhonda Byrne credits Esther with inspiring her book *The Secret*.

Inspired action, as the words imply, means to act appropriately and easily on the feedback you get. It's the vehicle that drives you to your goal after your GPS maps it. I have fabulous news for you: You get to choose the vehicle.

MYTHS THAT BLOCK THE RIGHT CHOICE

Many people, though, don't choose a vehicle capable of getting them to their destinations easily or at all; their beliefs misguide them. One of two common attitudes keep them from understanding and engaging the power of inspired action. These attitudes are myths. Followers of one myth believe that their thoughts and faith alone will bring about their desired outcome; the Universe will take care of the rest. Followers of the other myth discount the role of the Universe. They believe they must achieve everything by themselves, and they expect to struggle.

MYTH 1: "I DON'T NEED TO HELP THE UNIVERSE TO HELP ME"

This parable illustrates the fallacy of the first type of attitude. A man believed that the Universe would protect him no matter what. He had read in many books that the Universe is a safe place for those who focus on positive thoughts. His belief was so strong, in fact, that he didn't panic when the local dam broke. He trusted so powerfully in his safety that when the waters rose up to his second-floor apartment, he turned away each boat that came to rescue him.

Soon the water forced him to the roof, and he wondered why his faith hadn't saved him yet. He believed it would still happen, though, so when a helicopter hovered overhead to rescue him, he called out, "No, thank you—I'm safe! Go away."

The rescuers did as he asked, and he drowned in the flood. When he arrived in heaven, the man complained to God: "I believed that you love me and that you would protect me. Why didn't you?" God replied, "How can you say I didn't help you? I sent you boats and a helicopter!"

The man's GPS—his feedback—did its job, but he didn't take inspired action. Waiting for magic to happen, he was blind to the fact that it was already right there in front of him.

It's common to be blind, as I sometimes see in comments about one of my blog posts or videos. Thinking that the Universe will handle everything without any action on one's own part is like being a twig in the water. It's like being the floater you read about in the introduction. As every surfer knows, going with the flow is cool, but sometimes you also need to correct your course.

MYTH 2: "I MUST *SUFFER* TO SUCCEED"

The second type of person does believe in action, but not the inspired kind. They're sure they must struggle for everything they get. The movie *The Pursuit of Happyness*[2] glorifies the dangerous myth that it takes desperate struggle to succeed. Will Smith plays a homeless father who suffers to become a stockbroker while going through a divorce and raising a young son. Eventually, after going through hell, he succeeds.

If inspired action is like driving to your destination in a reliable vehicle, it's as if Will Smith's character and people like him choose to travel in a broken one. They believe in the value of only rough journeys. They're often the ones who work at jobs they hate and meet people they don't like. They're the ones who choose to struggle.

Are you driving a broken vehicle? When I ask my seminar participants to imagine themselves free to choose any car in a lot that contains many types—from reliable to broken—they don't think twice about choosing a reliable one. But the same people choose the broken one in real life because they—like so many people—have learned that life must be hard.

The struggles work out in the end, which implants the belief that they're the only route to success. People aren't

---

[2] That's really how the title is spelled.

searching for easy paths or the inspired action. They don't want the nice cars, because they believe only the broken ones can bring them the results they want.

MORE ABOUT OBSTACLES TO INSPIRED ACTION

The Pursuit of Happyness is far from alone in perpetuating the fallacies that life must be hard and that nothing that comes easily has value. Much literature and many movies, programs, and celebrity interviews reinforce those ideas. In fact, most movies are 99 percent struggle and 1 percent happy ending—if there's a happy ending at all. We're *raised* on these messages, and they only compound throughout our formative years. These messages program our subconscious minds.

Take most fairy tales. Cinderella, with no confidence or personal power, must struggle every day until *outside* forces come to rescue her. Many fairy tales also put forth the myth that rich people, presumably with easy lives, are villains. By the end of the stories, they get the punishment the stories suggest they deserve.

Later in your development, you watch superheroes and action-movie stars struggle on their way to a big win. No matter where you start watching any Bruce Willis movie, you can tell within seconds where you are in it by the amount of blood on the star's face. That's how all these movies go, and they have a big impact on the stories of *your* life.

People might also inherit the life-is-struggle idea from their parents. The parents themselves inherited it, and they believe it because that's how they've experienced life. They don't realize that they've experienced life that way *because* of their beliefs.

WHY WE BUY THE MYTHS

Our subconscious minds remain susceptible to the influence of these media-, movie-, and literature-induced myths, even in adulthood. Because tobacco companies understood and exploited the influential power of the media decades ago, they planted images of attractive smokers in movies, commercials, and print ads.

Such powerful images are able to program our minds and influence our beliefs because of the altered—entranced—mental state with which we consume them. Myths infect the mind like viruses, as malware infects computers.

Actor Denzel Washington believes in the myth that only struggle has value. During an NAACP Image Awards acceptance speech, he said, "Ease is a greater threat to progress than hardship."[3] He also made the point that if

---

[3] I agree that ease can kill passion, but for a different reason. Unlike Washington, I don't believe ease has no value.

success came easily, everyone would be successful. This is mostly bullshit. Hard work can and does produce results, but it's not the only way to achieve them. Washington could have achieved his success without the struggle if he had let go of his outdated model of the world.

Although Washington succeeded, many people who struggle and see life as a fight often give up too early. *That's* the reason most people fail, not because they didn't struggle enough. They see the world as only winners and losers. The common idea that people must fight for their happiness suggests that someone is trying to prevent it, and they're often right. *They* are fighting themselves and their beliefs.

The good news is that just as computers have antivirus programs, so do our minds. One way to protect yourself is to become aware of the damaging media messages you may passively consume. Another is to change your beliefs and learn that you don't need to struggle to attain your goals.

But even hard work doesn't have to involve struggle. I coach a seventeen-year-old hockey player who trains intensely against players who are five years older than he is. When I asked him whether hockey is a struggle for him, he laughed, "Hockey a struggle? Never! Repotting plants in my parents' garden—now *that's* a struggle!" He couldn't even imagine seeing what he loves as a struggle. Because it's his inspired action, playing hockey *gives* him energy.

INSPIRING ACTION: ENERGIZING, NOT EFFORTLESS, NEVER PAINFUL

As the young hockey player demonstrates, inspired action isn't necessarily effortless, but the effort gets easier when the energy investment pays back. When you release your energy into the world, you receive much more in return.

Investing energy is like planting a sunflower seed. If the timing and environment are right, the seed will grow into a flower that can hold as many as two thousand seeds. By anyone's standards, that's a terrific investment. So is going to the gym, in which sustained investment in energy produces much more.

The thing to remember, though, is that the effort should not be painful. Professional bodybuilders and athletes who live by the mantra of "No pain, no gain" often harm themselves at least in the long term. They mismanage their energy with illegal and harmful substances. We can't always choose our situations, but we can choose how we react to them, which in turn affects our energy levels.

Energy mismanagement was the problem for an office worker who approached me after a recent presentation I gave to the largest oil company in Slovakia. The worker asked how to feel energy in a job that exhausted and frustrated her so much that it gave her headaches.

I showed the worker that although she had no control over the company's choice of destination, she did control the choice of her metaphorical vehicle. She had chosen one in need of repair, so she had to push it. In fact, she had to struggle because she had engaged the emergency brake. She needed to choose a different vehicle by changing the way she feels about her job and finding passion for it. She needed inspired action.

Like many who come to my speeches and seminars, the worker believed that she needed to change her environment—in her case, her job. As I told her, "Changing the road won't help you move forward in a broken vehicle." Of course, sometimes the environment *does* need to change. More often, though, people come to realize that they just need to change how they act, behave, and feel about their environment.

RECOGNIZING PAINLESS PROGRESS

The mandatory-struggle myth is so pervasive that it doesn't occur to most people that they can achieve that mental shift. What also tends to happen is that the ones who do achieve progress aren't aware of it. When progress

CHANGING THE ROAD WON'T HELP YOU MOVE FORWARD IN A BROKEN VEHICLE.

isn't painful, people often don't recognize, acknowledge, or recall it, because it doesn't feel like progress to them.

I've learned I need to remind clients again and again of their progress and the fact that there can be progress without pain. I'm thinking of a client who had been in therapy for years before he contacted me with a desperate cry for help. His agoraphobia (fear of going outside) was so intense that he had been a patient in a psychiatric clinic—*nine times*. He told me he would kill himself before he would return.

After one two-hour meeting with him at his apartment, he began to change. For the first time in three-and-a-half years, he agreed to go outside; we took a walk together.

A month or so later, I asked him to measure his progress on a scale of minus-ten (horrible) to plus-ten (euphoric). He rated his starting point—when he had been afraid both of staying home by himself and of leaving his house—at minus-ten.

He gave himself credit for improvement and a score of plus-five only when he was in his apartment! He rated his outside progress still at minus-ten! I knew that wasn't true; since we had met, he had been outside every day and had visited the dentist, which he hadn't been able to do in years. Like so many other people, he felt that change could occur only in struggle and pain. His progress felt too easy for him to recognize.

I explained the concept of ease and that change didn't have to be hard. Only then could he recognize his progress, and he changed his outside assessment to plus-three. Today he not only goes outside, but he also plans to travel—a feat he could not have even imagined before.

Not only do many of us have to learn how to *recognize* our progress, but we also have to remember how to easily *make* it. Our forgotten ability to progress without pain or struggle is why I call children the most successful species on the planet. They demonstrate inspired action. They smile through failing and through achieving the most magical results, as we did when we were children. We learned tough tasks like walking, talking, eating, and dressing with ease because we didn't think of them as difficult.[4]

We simply *enjoyed* learning, both for the sake of it and for the fun of emulating adults. We learned through inspired action—by feeling good. We continued to see learning difficult tasks as fun until adults taught us that they were difficult.

We adults, though, believe it's difficult to learn a language.

---

[4] Adults who have to relearn to walk or talk after an illness or injury know how much effort it takes. They're more likely to perceive the effort as a difficult task than as an inspired action.

Yet we can actually learn languages a little more quickly than children can, at least according to *The Third Ear*, a book by Chris Lonsdale. The book is the result of a study that tracked families that immersed themselves in a new language by moving to the country where it was native.

HOW TO TAKE INSPIRED ACTION

To recapture what you once knew instinctively, practice focus—your most valuable asset. Applying focus has the greatest potential to change your reality. Focus on your dream and the life you expect to have after you achieve it.

When Denzel Washington talks about struggle, I think he really means staying in focus on a passion-linked purpose for as long as it takes. Don't force it, though. You can take inspired action only after you hear what the Universe is telling you through your GPS.

DO WHAT YOU *LOVE*

Your job is to take that action. Don't be like Cinderella and the many people who wait for happiness to come from outside. In the real world—and this is key—happiness is an inside job. To be happy and to take inspired action, do the things that make you happy. Invest your time on earth in doing what you're passionate about and what connects you to your purpose.

LOVE WHAT YOU DO

Choose your vehicle and your state of mind. Tasks are boring or stressful only if you decide they are. Consider that idea when you ask for a raise or do anything else you might dread. Reframe the task with good feelings.

I remind myself to practice what I teach. As an entrepreneur, I do many things I love—running seminars, writing blog posts, recording podcasts, and writing books. But like everyone, I also have to do what doesn't come naturally, including boring office procedures.

I didn't love performing those procedures until I taught myself to. Love transformed the once-dreaded tasks into inspired actions. I recommend that you also learn to love more tasks on the way to your dream. You don't need to love every task. Just stay open to it, and keep learning and experimenting.

"THE BIG CLAP THEORY"

You also need to focus on one thing at a time, which is all we can really do well. Unless you're a computer, multitasking is a fallacy. Not even people who pride themselves on their ability to multitask can actually do more than one thing at a time. What they're really doing is this: they're jumping from one task to another and rarely doing justice to any of them.

> YOU DON'T NEED TO LOVE EVERY TASK. JUST STAY OPEN TO IT, AND KEEP LEARNING AND EXPERIMENTING.

We often think we're multitasking when we're really just distracted, as what I call the "The Big Clap Theory" suggests. If you were to clap loudly beneath birds gathered in a tree, they would instantly fly away. If you stop, they might return. This is similar to how we respond to the many distractions in our own lives.

You know how it is. You start working on something when (clap!) the phone rings. You get back to work when (clap!) you wonder about your Facebook status. Then (clap, clap!) someone comes by to offer you coffee. Would you consciously permit someone else to clap away your dreams?

Internal clappers might also be distracting you. Many people have what I call a random-thought generator. Those random thoughts include worries and self-doubts. "Do I have enough likes on my Facebook page?" "Is it going to rain?" These thoughts distract you from taking conscious, inspired action toward your desired future. The more difficult or boring your task is, the more vulnerable you are to both external and internal distractions.

Many people these days are suffering from a shortened attention span. You can see movies and music videos reflecting and influencing this trend. People get bored if a camera angle exceeds a few seconds. Compare that to the slower-paced films of past eras. As the world moves faster and faster, our brains become conditioned to continue to seek new and more frequent impulses. We don't want to miss anything, so we become *addicted* to distraction, and it can drain us.

"If you cannot focus longer than ten minutes on your goal, or on your dream, then it probably isn't your dream." When German author Vera F. Birkenbihl said that line before the era of the web and mobile phones, it was easier to focus for that amount of time. These days, though, when we're conditioned to refocus our attention every few seconds, focusing requires more skill.

BECOME ADDICTED TO *FOCUS*

Children have the edge in their ability to focus, not only to painlessly learn. They can spend hours building sandcastles, playing their favorite games, and putting on plays. Much to many parents' regret, they can also focus on the same movie over and over again. Learn from them and from yourself as a child. On what inspired action did you focus for hours?

Another way to learn to avoid clappers is to start by noticing them in your daily life. Observe how often you let your favorite clappers distract you. If you find that you're addicted to distraction, you'll need to substitute an addiction to focus.

Identify—and consciously prepare to ignore—your distractions. If your phone distracts you, set your phone to "mute." Put your phone in a different room if you have to. If your least resistible distraction is email, "quit mail" or turn off alerts. Are people showing up to distract you? Take your work where they can't find you, or work while they sleep.

Focus is like a muscle. Practice avoiding distraction, and train your attention for longer and longer intervals.

THE HAPPY-ENDING STRUCTURE

Along with doing what you love, loving what you do, and focusing, inspired action also requires you to believe things will work out well. Also, make sure you end every encounter (with others or yourself) on a positive note.

This is not some bullshit mantra. Thinking positively and ending on a positive note are important for two reasons: You'll install great subconscious strategies, and you'll accelerate your learning process. That belief reinforces the wisdom of abandoning the idea of necessary struggle. For inspiration, look to *It's a Wonderful Life*,[5] which includes the longest, happiest ending I've ever seen in a film.

---

5   Directed by Frank Capra and starring James Stewart and Donna Reed (RKO Radio Pictures, 1946). Based on the short story *The Greatest Gift* by Philip Van Doren Stern.

HOW TO LET GO OF STRUGGLE: AN EXORCISM EXERCISE

To exorcise the myth that you need to struggle, revisit how you arrived at that notion with this exercise. Write down the names of three fictional characters who inspired or influenced you in your youth. Also write down their traits, including whether they struggled to reach their outcome.

Now notice which of those traits you may have adopted. Maybe your heroes, like mine, were Superman and the fairy-tale princes who struggled to killed dragons. When I did the exercise, I also noticed that they always work for free. Having such heroes might lead people to believe that they can do something they love or earn money from their work, but not both.

The Winnetou[6] movies, more of my youthful favorites, also reinforced that notion. Winnetou is an Apache chief who rides around saving the Wild West—no invoicing or money involved. In fact, those movies so influenced me when I was a kid that I went through a period without smiling much or showing any emotion because I wanted to be like my hero.

More potential influence—the fact that many of these heroes often remain single and mostly friendless—

---

6   The Winnetou movies, produced and released in the 1960s, were based on stories Karl May had written decades before.

might cause their young fans to grow up with the idea that dedication to a mission and loving relationships are mutually exclusive.

Until I learned the value of inspired action, I didn't like cleaning my partner's and my home, which I also lay at the feet of my movie heroes. I *never* saw them clean their rooms! I finally turned the activity into inspired action by combining it with listening to podcasts, dancing to music, or timing myself to beat my previous speed record.

I thought life equals struggle because Superman had to fight. But that message acted on me in reverse; for a while, I also equated struggle with achievement, so I didn't try to achieve anything. I began to achieve only when I became aware of the power of those influences, of inspired action, and of focus. Now I'm taking inspired action to achieve my goals and influence people toward ease and joy.

By understanding your influences and combining focus with inspired action, you can positively influence not only your life but also the lives of others. Consider it your *responsibility* to stay focused.

WHAT ELSE TO DO

All actions can be inspired; it's all in how you look at them. You can't always choose your tasks, but you can always choose your emotion and your level of inspiration. By focusing, you can *create* inspiration. To change your emotional state, make work fun, as children do with anything and as I do when I clean the house, calculate my taxes, or work out at the gym.

When you do change your emotional state, you'll create new connections in your brain that turn even mundane tasks into inspired actions. You don't need external resources. You can do the things you're doing now, just with an enlightened understanding and approach.

KEEP GROWING LIKE A TREE

Be like a tree, which keeps growing until it dies.[7] Recognize what you did in the past, and learn from your mistakes. Always ask yourself what's next, and how you can enjoy the process.

Be like Jaromír Jágr, who clearly does all that. Jágr is an active hockey player who's enjoying success in his mid-forties, an advanced age for a professional hockey player. When retired hockey legend Wayne Gretzky was fifty-six, he joked that if Jágr continues playing like that at *his* age, Gretzky might consider reactivating his own skates.[8]

---

7   Remember counting tree rings when you were a kid? Every year, a tree grows a new ring.

8   In 2017, Jágr moved to second place on the National Hockey League's All-Time Points Leaders list, after Gretzky.

YOU CAN'T ALWAYS CHOOSE YOUR TASKS, BUT YOU CAN ALWAYS CHOOSE YOUR EMOTION AND YOUR LEVEL OF INSPIRATION.

KISS YOUR COMFORT ZONE GOODBYE

Along with focusing, continuing to grow is also your responsibility to yourself and to the world. But you can't do it by remaining in your comfort zone. An English teacher didn't learn that lesson until she came to my seminar. She asked me how to start taking risks and gave evidence of her tendency to avoid them.

The teacher said she hadn't set her sights high enough when she chose her mate because she worried she wouldn't be able to keep a desirable one. She also mentioned turning down the offer of a coveted job because she feared she wasn't good enough. In every aspect of her life, she—like so many people—was afraid of failure. In avoiding risks that could lead to failure, though, she also avoided inspired action.

Cool things happen when you leave your comfort zone. Imagine going into a meeting with a client whom you want to persuade to contract your services but whom you expect to resist every idea. If you do what's familiar, he'll fight you as usual and you won't make the deal. Instead, you could see the encounter as an opportunity for flirting, not fighting, and I don't mean the romantic or sexual kind. See what happens when you treat him like a friend instead of like someone standing in your way. Make the meeting fun.

Your clients will keep the emotional memory of how you make them feel, not necessarily what you said. To prove that to yourself, think about a seminar or business meeting you attended two years ago. What do you recall? It's probably how you felt there more than what you heard. Think about how you can bring fun to all of your relationships, including business. The better you feel, the better people around you will feel. In turn, the better *they* feel, the more they will want to repeat the experience and be with you again.

FIND ENERGY MATCHES

You'll be more successful and happy if you can surround yourself with people who match your energy. Putting out positive, playful energy will attract people who will respond to it and with whom you can create inspirational interaction. This way you don't have to wear a mask in your business dealings, trying to be someone you're not. Whenever I don't feel that match with potential clients, I refer them to someone else.

You may be thinking, "That's great for you, Peter, but I can't choose the people I work with. I especially can't choose my boss!" Are you *sure*? How did you get into that situation? You took that job or that mate.[9] The people around you are your feedback. Listen to it, and act on it.

---

9   Esther Hicks even believes we choose our *parents*, but science can't help us prove that one.

RECOGNIZE WHAT YOU DID IN THE PAST, AND LEARN FROM YOUR MISTAKES. ALWAYS ASK YOURSELF WHAT'S NEXT, AND HOW YOU CAN ENJOY THE PROCESS.

Acting on it doesn't mean you have to leave the situation. Something must change, though—the environment or the people, or your response, which in turn will change the environment or the people. Use M.A.G.I.C., and ask yourself what you want instead. Consider how an optimal situation would look and feel.

A story by Karel Čapek, a Czech writer in the early 1900s, emphasizes the value of surrounding yourself with people who support you.[10] The story opens with a man, Mr. Tomsik, remembering the previous night's dream of flying like a bird. Now awake, walking on a Prague boulevard, he smiles at the thought of what it would be like to fly right now in real life.

Mr. Tomsik finds the street almost empty, so he decides to test his crazy idea. On his second attempt, he succeeds! He actually flies! For a while, he keeps his secret, quietly training and getting better and better. Then he decides that he needs to share his ability with the world. The first person he shows is his neighbor, a journalist who helps him arrange a demonstration in a stadium.

The experts gather on the day of the event. When Mr. Tomsik takes his first few steps, the experts yell, "Stop!

---

10 The story's title translates to "The Man Who Knew How to Fly." It's one of the "would-be" tales by Karel Čapek collected in an English translation by Norma Comrada: *Apocryphal Tales: With a Selection of Fables and Would-Be Tales* (North Haven, CT: Catbird Press, 1997).

THE PEOPLE AROUND YOU ARE YOUR FEEDBACK. LISTEN TO IT, AND ACT ON IT.

That isn't the right way to run!" One of the experts demonstrates. He starts again, now running their way, and he leaps into the air. Again he hears, "Stop!" This time, they advise him to change the way he leaps. It went on and on like this.

When he finished following all of this expert advice, he made a sad discovery: He could no longer fly—on this day or ever again.

Even if Mr. Tomsik ultimately couldn't choose who would share in his experience, he needed to stay true to his inspired action. The story also tells us that if you want to fly, surround yourself with people who can fly. Stay connected to people who inspire you and whom you inspire.

Steer clear of energy vampires, people who laugh at or shut down your ideas. They may be well-intentioned people who care about you and think they're helping you, but they're actually sucking your energy. You need every bit of your energy to invest in your dreams. You need your energy to focus and to take inspired actions.

YOU'RE READY TO FLY

At this point in the book, you've picked up all the principles you need to bring M.A.G.I.C. into your life to achieve your dreams, and those are the first four letters. The next chap-

IF YOU WANT TO FLY, SURROUND YOURSELF WITH PEOPLE WHO CAN FLY. STAY CONNECTED TO PEOPLE WHO INSPIRE YOU AND WHOM YOU INSPIRE.

ter will show you how to use them to create real change—to create your new reality.

CHAPTER 6

C–CREATE THE WAVES: CONSISTENT ACTION LEADS TO CONSTANT GROWTH

DO YOU KNOW WHAT THE FASTEST-GROWING plant in the world is? It's bamboo. In the right conditions, certain species can grow up to three feet a day. So, let's say you plant a bamboo seed, and you expect to see the results the next day. However, nothing happens for several days. You might be thinking, "It's not growing!"

Then one day you come by, and it's a small plant. The next day, it's taller than you are. How is this possible? The seed had started its work immediately. It was setting roots underground. You couldn't yet see the growth, but it was already happening.

Why am I telling you this? I'm talking about bamboo because it has a lot to teach us about consistency, the final step in the M.A.G.I.C. process.

You need consistency to experience the full effect of the Wave. In this context, it means that you need to do more than take one inspired action one time. Achieving your dreams requires you to *consistently* and constantly magnetize your purpose with passion, use all your senses and your GPS, and take inspired action—time after time, like continuous waves.

Consistency *creates* the Waves in your life, an infinite number of them. It makes the ocean you're learning to surf.

Take consistent action even when you can't notice any improvement. It's like going to the gym just once and seeing no results. That's okay! You don't need quick results to tell you it's useful to go to the gym.

Anyway, as you've seen in previous chapters, even when there *is* undeniable evidence, we're often the last ones to recognize *that* we've changed and by how much. It's not like seeing yourself in an actual mirror. If it were like that, and you were frowning at your reflection and assuming a defeated posture, of course you could see the difference when you brightened up.

Life is more like a *delayed* mirror. The change itself doesn't take a long time. Your new reflection of that change, though, will take time to reveal itself to you. How long? Nobody knows. However, M.A.G.I.C. helps you speed up the process. Be consistent in your new lifestyle, and eventually the mirror will reflect your new reality. Remember, life is a feedback mechanism.

When people don't see immediate growth, they often feel as though they're stagnating. That feeling causes them to abandon the action. Stagnation is an illusion, though. Nature shows us only two options: growth and decomposition. There's nothing in-between. The purpose of a tree is to grow, and once it fulfills that purpose, it decomposes. Unlike a tree, we can choose to thrive or decompose. Spend a week on the sofa, and you'll have less energy, not more. That's choosing decomposition.

Which will you choose?

HOW TO MAKE WAVES

Let me give an example of how combining consistency works with the other points of M.A.G.I.C. to achieve success. About four years ago, I was jogging in Bratislava between a deep lake and a fence that encircles a soccer field. The fence wasn't tall enough that day. One of the players kicked the ball over it and into the water.

REMEMBER, LIFE IS A FEEDBACK MECHANISM.

The impish part of me thought, "Cool! Somebody's going to have to get wet now."

To my surprise, no one set foot into the lake. Instead, the players started searching on the ground for something. Now I was thinking, "Ah, they're looking for a long stick."

I was wrong again. They picked up small rocks and started throwing them into the lake. "What are they doing?" I thought. Then I realized, "Oh, that's genius! They're throwing the rocks beyond the ball." By doing so, the players created currents that pushed the ball back toward the shore where they could reach it. They demonstrated consistent inspired action!

That moment was a huge lesson for me. It presented an insight into the way the world could work if we let it. I'm so grateful that I witnessed it. I realized I had limited my expectation of their process to what I would've done. I must admit that the worst part of me had looked forward to someone getting wet, but the players gave me a far greater gift.

In addition to reinforcing the idea of M.A.G.I.C., the incident showed the need to consistently learn from others and stay open because lessons take place around us all the time. The players had solved their problem within twenty seconds *without* getting wet by demonstrating all the M.A.G.I.C. principles:

- First, the soccer players were clear on their goals. They knew exactly what they wanted—to get their ball back so they could continue to play. That's when they could engage the M.A.G.I.C.:
    - **M**: Their passion for playing the game magnetized their purpose.
    - **A**: They used all their senses to visualize the weight and size of the ball to help them figure out how to get it back.
    - **G**: They obviously set their GPS with values such as joy, creativity, and fun.
    - **I**: They took inspired action. There was no struggle and no blaming anyone for the ball's location. They made a game out of it.
    - **C**: They created the Wave by being consistent in their actions.

HOW TO MAKE WAVES IN YOUR LIFE

The soccer ball example also shows that no single M.A.G.I.C. step will work without the others. You need to apply them all, you need to enjoy the process, and again, you need to do it all consistently. So, now it's your turn to create Waves that push your goals within your reach and without struggle. Listen to your heart while you follow the steps. The more you do it, the better you'll understand how the model works. Take M.A.G.I.C. out for a spin on your own goals. Why not today?

For encouragement and inspiration, recall Rado from the introduction, who sustained a spine injury that paralyzed him from the neck down. His M.A.G.I.C. practice disproved the doctors who didn't expect him to be able to ever move below his neck. Before we worked together, his goal was only to not have to depend on his assistant for everything.

I taught Rado to expand his goals and to express them in positive terms. The process brought him clarity when he discovered that what he really wants is to walk again, drive his car, and have a wife and children.

Here's exactly how M.A.G.I.C. worked for him:

M: We **M**agnetized Rado's clear purpose with his passion for being an athlete, a passion he thought his spinal-cord injury had destroyed. One of our first steps was to change the way he looked at himself. When he could see himself as an athlete again, he could *be* one, even in the wheelchair. He's now the athletic director of a handball club, where he helps to motivate players.

A: Because the subconscious understands **A**ll senses, my partner and I trained Rado to visualize while engaging them all. To program his mind for success, he focused on the end result, not the intervening steps, and he did it consistently.

Rado visualized the sight of himself walking and driving again in vivid detail, including colors. He could see himself looking down at his legs as they moved. He visualized what his footsteps and car engine sounded like and what it felt like to move his body, use his legs, and hold the steering wheel. He visualized the smells of his car and the smells and taste of the food that he would be able to feed himself. He could even have visualized the taste and feel of the champagne with which he would toast his achievements.

The more Rado visualized, the more use of his body he regained. I'm not a doctor, but as I understand it, he created new neural connections.

G: We also programmed Rado's **GPS** to ensure that he kept moving toward his goals, not away from them. Misdirection is always a risk, and it was particularly true in his case. The accident had depressed him to the point that he no longer wanted to live.

The feedback the GPS delivered, especially when he did physical therapy, was all painful. He focused on the pain and looked at these exercises as something he must do, not wanted to do. He didn't do them with his heart, and that attitude dramatically slowed his progress.

When, instead, Rado wondered how he could make those exercises more fun, he had a breakthrough.

I: The thought led to his **I**nspired action. One of the ways to add inspired action is laughter, and that's what Rado added. From that moment on, while he exercised, he began to laugh out loud. At first, his devoutly Christian father thought his son had gone crazy; when he heard the laughter coming out of Rado's room, he crossed himself.

C: Rado **C**onsistently applied all the model's steps, including laughter and a mental anchor (see the box) as a source of energy. When he exercised, he imagined stepping into a beam of light.

M.A.G.I.C. helped Rado to create the Waves that led to the M.A.G.I.C. moment when he relearned how to drive.

HOW "ANCHORING" SUPPORTS M.A.G.I.C.

Rado, who was paralyzed from the neck down, eased the pain of his physical therapy by connecting laughter to what had been an ordeal. In doing so, he installed in his brain what neuro-linguistic programming (NLP) practitioners call "anchors." These are activities or thoughts chosen to combine with current circumstances to create a desired state of mind. *Using* anchors, once they're installed, is called "firing" them.

Your brain already holds perhaps thousands of anchors that connect to your feelings even if you didn't know to call them that. They may include beautiful images of your loved ones' faces, holiday scenes, your wedding day, or the births of your children. You can engage them even without looking at an actual picture of them. They're like a mental photo album. You can create anchors for any of your five senses. Something as simple as pressing together your fingers or touching a certain part of your body (like your shoulder) can be an example of a kinesthetic anchor. Laughter is mostly auditory and kinesthetic.

Smells can also be powerful anchors. The entire perfume industry depends on that fact. Beyond that, some fashion companies use the same fragrance in all their stores so they can install and fire olfactory anchors. The companies know the scent will subconsciously influence customers' behavior. Advertisers in general go to great lengths to associate positive feelings with their brands because they know the power of anchors to change people's emotions.

To be able to laugh at all, Rado had to relearn how to feel joy and gratitude. You might wonder how he could feel grateful, given what had happened to him. At first, he wondered too. Then he thought about all the people who helped him every day. If he could remember how to feel joy and gratitude, so can you. No matter what your circumstances are, you can change how you feel about them.

HIGHER-MISSION WAVES FOR A BETTER WORLD

All the M.A.G.I.C. model's steps support consistency. Finding what you love and taking inspired action make it easier to continue than to stop. When you magnetize your purpose, also consider whether and how it can improve the lives of people around you. A purpose with a higher mission dramatically enhances those lives.

Dreaming of owning your favorite car is certainly nice. On the other hand, what does it do for the world? "All about me" thinking made the world what it is today. That type of thinking has to change because it's not sustainable. Asking yourself how you can contribute to real change is where real M.A.G.I.C. happens.

I do everything in my power to contribute. My dream is that I can continue to create Waves and encourage everyone who learns of this work to do the same. I think of having a higher mission as a triple-win strategy. In the conclusion to this book, I'll explain that idea.

M.A.G.I.C. RESOURCES

If you're still wondering how you can make M.A.G.I.C. happen in your life, the answer is to tap into the resources you've had access to all along. You've already used them. M.A.G.I.C. has brought you where you are today—to every achievement, big and small, in your past and present life.

Maybe now you have a goal of finding yourself, but I don't think that's the right goal. I deeply believe that life is about *creating*, not finding, yourself. The question is this: What type of person do you want to be? That doesn't mean denying who you are or wearing a mask. Instead, it means creating the most beautiful version of yourself.

Not using the unlimited M.A.G.I.C. available to you to create yourself is like being a grand piano with only three keys. When a piano technician adds the other keys, now the piano is able to play all the melodies and symphonies of the world, not only the simplest tunes. It is the same piano, but now it has infinite ability to express itself. By applying M.A.G.I.C., you can do the same.

MAGIC QUESTIONS

- How can I create Waves to ride to my dreams?
- How can I create more consistency in my life?
- What's my next step?
- Where can I experience more joy?
- How can my passionate actions help people?

CONCLUSION

HEADING FOR THE TRIPLE WIN

YOU'VE NO DOUBT HEARD the expression "Knowledge is power." I don't agree with that idea. Knowledge alone is useless. Power really lies in *applying* it. Don't be like the many people who don't take advantage of what they know. The knowledge you've gained in this book is only as good as what you do with it. You also have to apply the knowledge to know its value.

HOW TO KNOW THE M.A.G.I.C. IS WORKING

As you've seen in previous chapters, you might not be sure you're changing even when you apply the knowledge. You'll need to look for the Waves in your life. I can't tell you exactly what those look like, because they change according to the person and the situation. Whatever form they take, though, if you know to look for them, you recognize them the moment they arrive.

When you look back on your life, maybe you can already pinpoint the presence of Waves. Maybe you can recall people, signs, or events coming into your life that helped you understand and achieve something. The Waves have always been there, whether or not you recognized them.

It may help you to recognize Waves in your life if you hear about a few of mine. When I conceived this book, I questioned how people would react to the word *magic* (in the titles of the model and of this book). I also wondered whether I should use the word at all. For one thing, it's an English word that is not used in my country.

I continued to ponder the word while I walked down a street in my neighborhood in Bratislava, where my answer came in the form of a Wave. When a big yellow bus turned the corner in front of me, I saw these English words painted on its side: "Magic Tours." I laughed out loud at the form my answer took.

Another Wave accompanied this book. When I decided to publish it in the United States, I started to receive invitations to speak before US audiences although I hadn't told anybody my plan.[1]

---

[1] Sorry, Mom!

Of course, Waves apply everywhere, not just to books, as you saw with the soccer ball example from Chapter Six. Start applying M.A.G.I.C. in your own life, and watch the Waves come in.

PLAY A GAME TO TEST M.A.G.I.C.

You might want a quicker indication that the Universe is listening and responding. You can prove it with this game I invented. I call it "Space Ping-Pong," and you'll see why. I decided to test the Universe one day when I was sitting by the front window in a London restaurant and a little bored.

I asked the Universe to send me, one at a time, people of various descriptions. Every time I specified someone, the Universe immediately responded. A person of that specific type would walk by the window. I thought I had finally asked for too much when I asked for a tiger because the Universe didn't respond right away.

After twenty seconds, though, there she was: a woman in a tiger-striped dress. That return demonstrates the Universe's practical side. It was easier to deliver a dress than an exotic species. It also showed that the Universe has a sense of humor. The response's form won't always be exactly what you expect. The game reminds you to be playful and open—conducive states for inspired action.

At first, *I* wasn't entirely open to the M.A.G.I.C. at work in Space Ping-Pong. The skeptical side of me wondered whether the Universe would be able to return the ping-pong ball in a less diverse environment than a busy street in London. So I tested that; the game has worked everywhere I've played it.

Readers of my first book,[2] where I introduced Space Ping-Pong, have confirmed that the game works for them too. One man, for example, wrote that it produced several deer in a local forest where, in twenty years, he had never seen even one. The sighting converted him from a skeptic to a believer.

M.A.G.I.C. NEVER ENDS

The game satisfies our desire for instant gratification. M.A.G.I.C. works best, though, when you're in it for the long haul. Like waves in the sea, M.A.G.I.C. work is constant. Adopt it as your lifestyle, not as a quick fix, because it doesn't work that way. I welcome your contact, but don't write me that you've been trying for two weeks and nothing has happened. If nothing has happened, it's *because* you haven't made it your lifestyle.

---

2   *TRIUMF: Váš nový životný príbeh* (published in Slovakia in 2014). To find out when its English translation, *Triumph: Your New Life Story*, will be released in the United States, sign up for my newsletter at www.wavesofmagic.com.

You should continue to grow throughout your life. This book will help. I hope it has raised new questions for you. I also hope that each answer leads to more questions—each at a deeper level and with many more questions than answers. In fact, you'll never finish this work. You shouldn't even aspire to finish it, because doing so would signal the end of growth. Finishing the work would mean the end of curiosity, which itself can help with anything from depression to phobia. It may be no accident that the word *curiosity* has *cure* in it.

GO FOR THE TRIPLE WIN

My dreams for you are continued growth, as well as curiosity, happiness, and success. I want you to be the most beautiful version of yourself. I want that for you for your sake, as well as for my sake and that of the rest of the world. I deeply believe that when you change your life and when you take inspired actions, especially playful ones, you emit radiant, healing energy to the world.

Every time *that* happens, you've achieved what I call the "triple win." You've heard of a *win-win situation*, a term often applied to what happens when both parties in an interaction get what they want. The triple win favors not only both parties, but also the world. Let me explain:

Win 1: Sharing the principles in this book improves my life.

Win 2: Applying those principles improves *your* life.

Win 3: Improving our lives also could improve the lives of the people around us *even if they don't read this book*. You could inspire them exactly as the soccer players in the previous chapter inspired me.

The soccer players also scored a triple win, although they don't know it. They were able to keep playing soccer, no one got wet, and by observing the incident, I could share its power with you. That's the beauty of this work. The players' use of the M.A.G.I.C. principles might influence thousands of lives.

The world is watching you too. Be that role model. Imagine how many lives you can affect with yours.

THANK YOU, AND YOU'RE WELCOME TO MORE

I'm grateful to you for reading this book and being open to its lessons. As I've written it, I've applied the M.A.G.I.C. principles—feeling good and imagining you reading it. I invite you to test the principles and take action. If this book brought you energy and inspiration, I welcome you to learn more. Help yourself to bonus material and say hello at www.wavesofmagic.com. I'd love to hear from you.

I also suggest that you consider expanding your learning

with in-person training. I deeply believe in this book's ability to impart M.A.G.I.C. principles and spur you to action. The book includes great advice on applying those principles. You might find, though, that you need more help. I understand, and I encourage you to seek it. It's wise to ask for help. Only the foolish think they know it all.

What's more, as valuable as books are, I don't think anyone can become, say, a great tennis player by only reading a book. You also need to *play* tennis, and you benefit from direct and competent feedback on your strokes.

WHERE WILL M.A.G.I.C. LEAD YOU?

Join me again where this book began—at the seashore. The waves keep coming, one after another, full of fighters, floaters, and surfers. Which one will you be?

Be the surfer. Ride those Waves. You owe it to yourself and to the world.

ABOUT THE AUTHOR

PETER SASÍN is a public speaker and seminar presenter, the author of the best-selling book *Triumph: Your New Life Story*, and a licensed and certified trainer of Neuro-Linguistic Programming. He has created multiple methods that help people quickly achieve astonishing results, helping his clients change their behaviors and beliefs about the world and themselves, and discover who they are at their core. Peter specializes in high-performance coaching, changing belief systems in mere minutes. Among his clients are top business leaders, professional athletes, artists, and people like you.

www.ingramcontent.com/pod-product-compliance
Lightning Source LLC
Chambersburg PA
CBHW032121090426
42743CB00007B/420